Textile Travels

Textile
Travels

Anne Kelly

BATSFORD

First published in the United Kingdom in 2020 by
Batsford
43 Great Ormond Street
London
WC1N 3HZ

An imprint of Pavilion Books Company Ltd

ISBN 978-1-84994-564-6

A CIP catalogue record for this book is available from the British Library.

10 9 8 7 6 5 4 3 2 1

Reproduction by Rival Colour Ltd, UK
Printed and bound by Toppan Leefung Printing Ltd, China

This book can be ordered direct from the publisher at www.pavilionbooks.com

Page 1: Anne Kelly, *Environmental* (detail), mixed-media textile.

Page 2: Anne Kelly, *Japanese Kettles* (detail), mixed-media textile.

Opposite: Anne Kelly, *Sweet Box*, crayon drawing.

Contents

meet with it aga[...]
likely to meet wi[...]
dish of them.

On the damp grou[...]
there is a small mat of a [...]
that appears to escape the [...]
walk over it. It is know[...]
annual plant related to the sta[...]
which we found growing by [...]
ago. The stems of our tiny plan[...]
a few inches long and of a reddish[...]

1. Painted Lady; 2. Red Admiral; 3. Adonis Blue male;
4. Adonis female.

Automnal Butterflies.

Introduction

'Travel is fatal to prejudice, bigotry and narrow-mindedness.'

Mark Twain, American writer and humorist

Travel has been a central feature of my work and this book is by extension a continuation of the themes explored in my previous books *Textile Nature* and *Textile Folk Art*. I have always admired my adopted country's predilection for travel and exploration. In my solo and collaborative project work, travel has shaped and directed the themes, materials and outcomes of my textiles. At the same time, it has helped me to question and research the landscape, culture and traditions of the places I have visited and my surroundings closer to home.

Travel features heavily in textile art, whether it is a guild member making a 'travelling book', or a large installation mapping coastal erosion and the effects of climate change. As artists, travelling helps us to locate our place in the world and share our practice with new audiences. There is much to learn from different cultures and textiles are the residue of that education, also contributing to our identity as textile artists.

As part of my practice, museums and collections are always a great resource for making work. Celebrating and being inspired by what has been made in the past and understanding how it influences current makers can also be a part of the learning process. I have featured some wonderful exhibitions and collections in this book and my interpretations of work from them.

Chapter 1: Mapping the Journey looks at maps and ways of using them in textile artwork.

Chapter 2: Heading South looks at the influence of southern cultures on textile art, from Peru to India, via Australia, New Zealand, China and Italy. Traditional motifs and techniques engage new audiences while celebrating their rich cultural heritage.

Native Canadian and American cultures offer a huge variety of imagery and source material for textile artists. Work made referencing them can provide new insights into their purpose and this will be explored in **Chapter 3: Due North.**

Chapter 4: Stopping Places captures the moments in time on a journey that are distilled and remembered. A seaside hotel, a railway journey or a walk on the downs can all be the basis for a single piece or a series of work.

In **Chapter 5: Space and Exploration**, we will look at how imagination plays a big part in creativity, and connecting with the themes of space and boat travel will both be explored in this chapter. Visually, the moon and sky can be arresting, and it is fascinating to see how different makers interpret this. Sails and boats use textile in their construction and they are a popular theme for textile artists to portray in their work.

The final short section of the book, entitled **Resources for Journeys**, focuses on organizing materials and ideas before, during and after a journey, whether you are close to home or enjoying an adventure far away. By collating paper, fabric and stitch, we are able to condense and preserve memories, making observations and new, meaningful work. By understanding elements of our world near and far we can better portray, preserve and protect it.

Above: Festival of Britain map, hand embroidery from kit, UK 1950s, collection of Judith Mansfield, Todmorden Books. The symbols for the different areas of the UK are simplistic and nostalgic, yet the piece works as a whole without any signage, apart from the title and to indicate where London is.

Opposite: Travel collage with the author as a young artist.

Chapter 1

Mapping the Journey

'I've always been fascinated by maps and cartography. A map tells you where you've been, where you are, and where you're going – in a sense it's three tenses in one.'

Peter Greenaway, British film director

Anne Kelly, *Map Inspiration Box*, mixed media.

Mapping

I am sitting on a train, looking out of the window, thinking about the landscapes, towns and hamlets we are passing by. How do I begin to convey or portray this in cloth, and how do I tell the stories of the lives of the people and the histories of the places seen? A good start is to begin with a map, which can be many things. It is always an interpretation, no matter how true to life. Cartographers make a series of decisions about representation to create a map that we can read easily. In this sense, map-making is allied to drawing – another translation from three dimensions to a flat image.

In this chapter, we will look at how to use and make maps in your work in a creative and meaningful way. Old maps can be a source of information about the history of an area but they are also beautiful objects in themselves. I favour the old Ordnance Survey maps that can be found in charity shops and second-hand bookshops, as they have a scrim backing which makes them easier to cut and manoeuvre. In my *Map Tin Boxes* project, I used an old map of Paris, found in a French *brocante* shop, to line the tins with before adding the stitched elements.

I have used maps in a variety of ways in my work and will be exploring some of these in this chapter, as well as returning to them later on in the book. I also wanted to see how maps can be interpreted and act as an inspiration for contemporary work for a range of other textile artists.

Anne Kelly, *Map Tin Boxes* (open), mixed media in tin boxes.

Maps as images and as guides

» Lines

» Railways

» Airports

» Contours

» Seas

» Lakes

» Rivers

» Mountains

» Parks

» Forests

» Plains

» Paper maps

» Postcards

Anne Kelly, small
unframed works on
paper, mixed media.

Making Map Tin Boxes

Source some old tin boxes from charity shops or online. I used old stock cube, medicine and sweet tins, which I had long been collecting but was unsure of what to use them for.

1 Clean and dry the tins thoroughly. Some of the rusty or worn elements can be part of their charm, but you don't want them to have jagged edges or to be disintegrating.

2 Line the tins with paper or thin cloth. I used an old map sourced on a trip to Paris, gluing it into position with a glue stick and then varnishing it with acrylic varnish, although a diluted PVA mixture could be used.

3 Choose some stitched elements to go on the outside of the tins. I cut out some small pieces from scraps of vintage embroidery. These were then glued into place and varnished as in step 2.

4 Finally, choose a suitable sized piece of embroidery to place inside the tin, so it is visible when opened. I used some existing work that I wanted to showcase, and I made a paper template to fit the space before pinning it to the embroidery and cutting it out.

5 Glue your work into place and varnish the whole piece, inside and out. You may wish to leave the interior embroidery unvarnished, depending on the look you want.

Above: Anne Kelly,
Map Tin Boxes
(closed), mixed media.

Opposite: Anne Kelly,
Map Tin Boxes (open),
mixed media in tin
boxes.

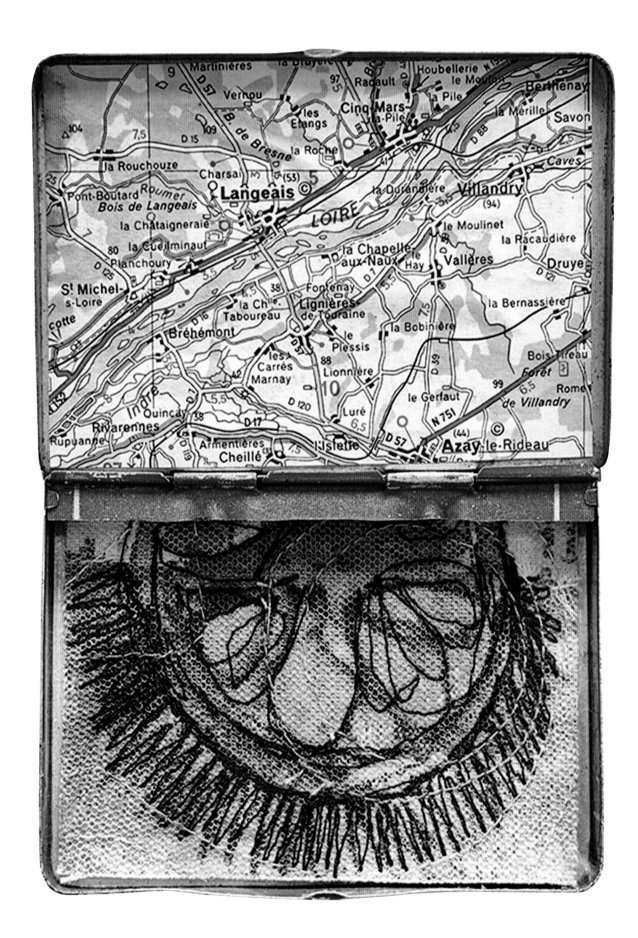

Hannah Streefkerk: Manual Repair

Hannah Streefkerk is a Sweden-based artist working with nature and place to create a remarkably textural map of the world. Hannah describes her ongoing project as follows:

'I embroider a map filled with lichen. In daily life people are often in a hurry and feel stressed. There is no time to pay attention to the smaller details around us. Details such as lichen are often taken for granted and hardly watched. Lichen are very interesting organisms, [the product of] a symbiotic relation between different kinds of algae and fungi. Lichen are good indicators of how the environment is doing. Clean air is needed for lichen to grow, so in places where you see a lot of lichen, the air is not polluted.'

'My works consist of installations *in situ*, outside or inside, and embroidered pieces. In a lot of my works, textiles and textile techniques, like crocheting and embroidery, play a significant role. I use a lot of time-consuming handcrafts and I always embroider by hand. This is important to me because it illustrates the nature of time in my work. Nature has a certain rhythm, whether it is changing with the seasons or in the course of a single day. This rhythm is visible; seasonal changes can be seen and my latest work relates to the passing of time in nature and to the cyclical nature of time.'

Hannah 'manually repairs' her natural surroundings, and emphasizes details in nature with needle and thread. She creates a visual metaphor for our responsibility for taking better care of our environment.

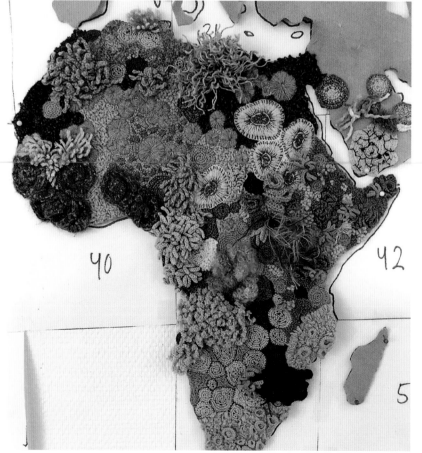

Left: Hannah Streefkerk, *Africa* (work in progress), mixed-media textile.

Above: Hannah Streefkerk, *Africa* (detail), mixed-media textile.

Vanessa Barragão: Botanical Tapestry

Vanessa Barragão is a Portuguese tapestry artist based near Porto. She develops wool and dyed yarn collections for use in her work through an eco-friendly artisanal process. Her connection with the landscape, and the sea in particular, can be seen in her work. She creates environments by combining craft and recycled materials into sculptural carpets and tapestries.

Above: Vanessa Barragão, *Botanical Tapestry*, mixed-media tapestry, *in situ* at Terminal 2, Heathrow Airport, London.

Inset: Vanessa Barragão, *Botanical Tapestry* (work in progress), mixed-media tapestry.

'The *Botanical Tapestry*,' she explains, 'is an artwork developed to celebrate the partnership between London's Heathrow Airport and Kew Gardens,' so linking the themes of travel and map making. 'Installed in the departure forecourt of Terminal 2, Heathrow Airport, this tapestry is 100 per cent handmade, using ancestral techniques like latch hook, crochet and felt needle. It took more than 520 hours to weave, using 8kg (18lb) of jute and cotton and 42kg (93lb) of recycled wool. This art piece represents the world map. There are visible all the colours present in our continents and oceans and some threatened species, like the coral reefs, and some plants around the world.'

Kate Tarling: A Sense of Place

Kate Tarling is an embroidery artist from Bristol in the south-west of England whose work illustrates how looking at places closer to home can also be inspirational. In her artwork *Bath*, Kate has managed to create a pictorial representation of the landscape in her neighbouring city through her instinctive use of colour and by creating texture with stitch. She describes her process for creating her maps:

> 'The inspiration for them comes from a desire to recreate a place, stitch it down permanently and capture a moment. Our surroundings are always changing but these textile maps are a fixed reminder of our place in time. I make them by painting onto a cotton or linen fabric and then stitching on top using freehand machine embroidery.
>
> 'I read human geography at university many years ago and my current textile work is heavily influenced by those studies, as my maps are all about a sense of place and stitching memories into a landscape.'

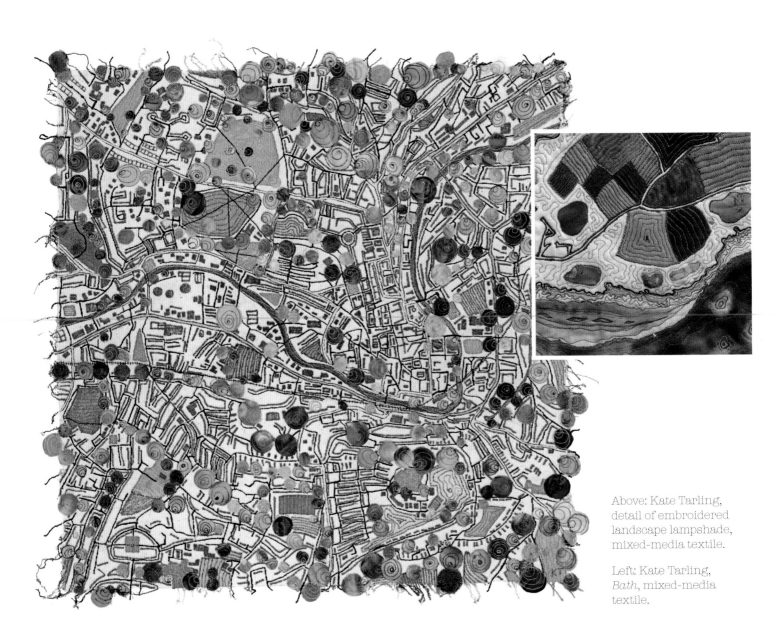

Above: Kate Tarling, detail of embroidered landscape lampshade, mixed-media textile.

Left: Kate Tarling, *Bath*, mixed-media textile.

London Collar Case

I found this case in a vintage shop in London, and wanted to make a repository for my work about London. I have a strong connection to the city and have happy memories of visits there when I was a child. My grandmother lived in north London and I always associate her house with lace, so it was a natural fit to make *London Collar Case*. I covered the case with a stitched collage, made from a tourist tea towel, and two found vintage lace collars. Inside the case, I have covered the lining around the handle with old London map pages and used it to store maps, folding books and ephemera associated with the theme.

Anne Kelly, *London Collar Case* (front), mixed-media textile on vintage case.

Making a Covered Case

F irst find a robust case. It can be made of any material, but should be clean and free from any heavily raised ornamentation.

1 To prepare your case for covering more easily, you may decide to remove extraneous buckles or straps by cutting or unpicking them.

2 To cover the sides of your case, first make templates to fit from newspaper, greaseproof paper or baking parchment. Then find fabric, or make pre-stitched panels large enough, to cover all the sides of the case.

3 Pin your templates to the pieces of fabric and cut them out carefully. It is always best to make them a bit larger than necessary as the panels can stretch or move while you are attaching them.

4 Attach the panels to the case – I use a small glue gun to do this – then cover each side with a layer of a 50/50 mixture of PVA glue and water to seal and protect the textile.

5 Add your finishing touches. I wrapped a twill trim around the handle, again using a glue gun to secure the ends and coating it in a diluted PVA mixture. I added part of a measuring tape along the top edge. I trimmed the edges and corners with canvas scraps, but you can use any ribbon or trim, or cut fabric that suits your piece.

Anne Kelly, *London Collar Case* (reverse), mixed-media textile on vintage case.

Ekta Kaul: Story Maps

One place can inspire very different approaches. Contrast Ekta Kaul's depiction of London with that of Richard McVetis, opposite. Describing her *Story Maps*, Ekta says:

'My embroidered, cartographic, wall-hung quilts seek to tell personal stories of place through maps. My creative voice is rooted in the plural – a unique assimilation of my Indian heritage and British training. I initially trained in Textiles and Clothing at India's National Institute of Design. Following this, I won two scholarships to pursue MA Textiles studies in the UK. A minimalist at heart, I draw inspiration from graphic aerial photography, vintage maps and gardens. I'm inspired by Zen gardens of Japan, calligraphy and architecture. My process is very much rooted in drawing and mark-making, and my work explores contemporary expressions of stitch using age-old techniques of hand embroidery, hand dyeing and block printing, and free machine embroidery.'

Ekta's work has been exhibited widely in London and internationally, and she has been releasing some of her designs as kits to make them more accessible to practitioners.

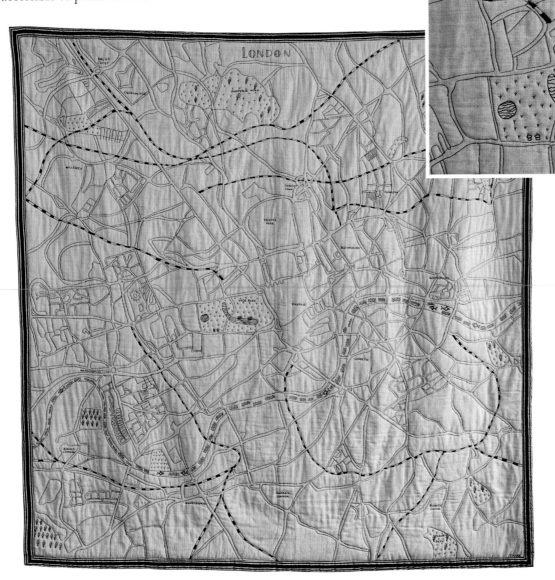

Above: Ekta Kaul, *London Map* (detail), mixed-media textile.

Left: Ekta Kaul, *London Map*, mixed-media textile.

Richard McVetis: Marking Time

Richard McVetis is a London-based textile artist and tutor, working with small and detailed stitches on a variety of surfaces. Describing his work, he says:

> 'The mapping of space and marking time and form are central themes. Ideas are often developed in response to, or created specifically to a moment, visualizing and making this a tactile and tangible object. The pieces created explore how objects, materials and places, through the action of hands, bear witness to the passing of time, of the mundane and monotonous regularity of everyday existence. I am interested in how a process can reveal a world seen from within, from a scale that can tell us much more about ourselves, about our trajectories in space, our interactions, and networks of processes that act as a catalyst for transformation within our lives.'

In *London Light Abstraction*, Richard worked from aerial photographs of the city at night, depicting the pattern created by humans and their interaction with the landscape at a macro scale. He says, 'Visualization of cities at this vantage point underlines the reshaping of our relationship to the urban environment.' Using hand embroidery, he records time through multiples of dots, lines and crosses. Meticulously drawn and stitched, his work reflects a preoccupation with the repetitive nature of a process, exploring the subtle differences that emerge through ritualistic and habitual making.

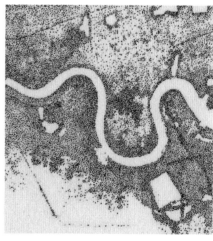

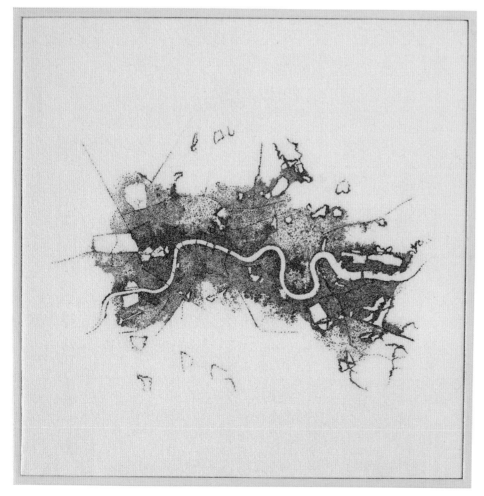

Above: Richard McVetis, *London Light Abstraction* (detail), hand embroidery and cotton on wool.

Left: Richard McVetis, *London Light Abstraction*, hand embroidery and cotton on wool.

London Satchel

The once-forgotten work of Brighton-born MacDonald (Max) Gill (1884–1947) was recently celebrated at Ditchling Museum of Art + Craft (East Sussex, England). Max Gill, younger brother of Eric, was a well-known illustrator, letterer, map-maker, architect and decorative artist in his day. He had a humorous and playful approach to his illustrative work. He was commissioned by a variety of institutions and organizations to visualize and document the rise of new (at that time) technologies like electricity, flying and radio broadcasting. His colourful work, with its distinctive Art Deco flourishes and tones, was popular and his best-known piece, the large 1914 *Wonderground Map*, was hung at every London Underground station. I covered this satchel (using similar techniques to my *London Collar Case*) as an homage to Max's map, and because it is reminiscent of the satchels that bus conductors used to carry on London buses.

Anne Kelly, *London Satchel*, mixed-media textile on vintage satchel.

London Toys

Inside *London Satchel* is a small book that I made a long time ago called *London Toys*, based on the small metal die-cast toys of London buses, taxis and letterboxes that were once common in souvenir shops. I also made a woodblock carving of a London bus, which is included here.

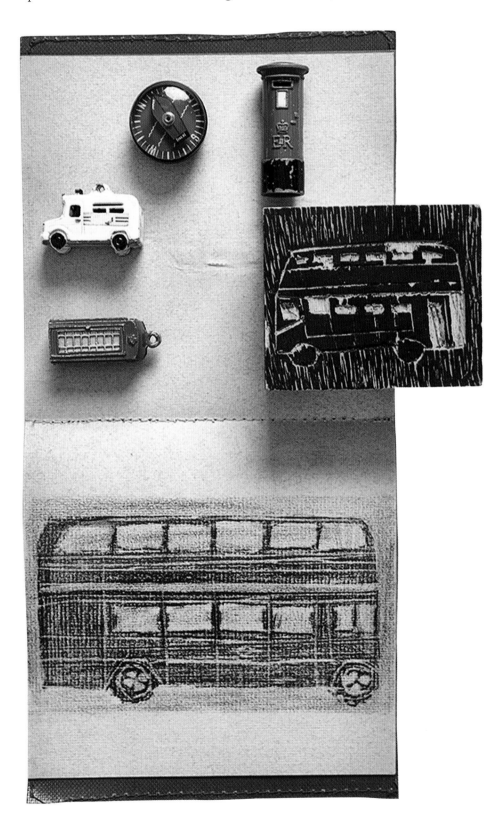

Anne Kelly, *London Toys*, block-printed folding book, wax rubbings from carved woodblocks, metal die-cast London toys, collection of the author.

Heidi Hankaniemi: Metro

Continuing with the city transport theme, we have Heidi Hankaniemi's *Metro* collection. Heidi is a Finnish-born, New York-based artist who combines a multi-disciplinary practice with an interest in the everyday and quotidian, looking to interpret narratives from these activities and domestic habits and paths. Describing the collection, she says:

> 'The act of sewing – piercing the fibres – allows me to create both a physical and an emotional bond with the fabric. It creates a connection between materials and their origins, and enables me to merge with them. While living in Oslo, Norway, I backstitched six subway maps and it felt fascinating to use an intimate, slow technique to describe large-scale, high-speed public transport systems.'

> 'I then stitched some more maps; the cities I'd visited, would like to visit, cities friends had been to … Eventually, eight years later, the project covered all the subway maps in the world, 148 of them. *Metro* is a travelogue, a stitch-by-stitch journey through every subway in the world. I've worked on the maps on and off for over a decade, while living in different countries. It's a diary in motion, about motion. I stitched Cairo on a train in Norway, Moscow on my way to Toronto, and so on … The metros themselves are in a constant flux, being reconstructed and redesigned.'

> 'The maps are based on the real-life pocket maps, with the correct colours and lines at the time of my journey through them. The maps are presented anonymously, without stations. They appear as abstract drawings, clusters of sewn lines in the air, but contain millions of lives making connections in the world. *Metro* has since been exhibited worldwide including in Russia, Finland and the USA.'

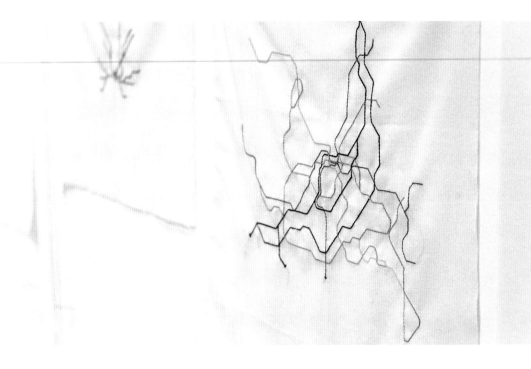

Above: Heidi Hankaniemi, *Metro*, mixed-media textile.

Left: Heidi Hankaniemi, *Metro*, mixed-media textile, *in situ*.

Devon Map

I found an old map of Devon in a charity shop and thought it would be a good way of combining textile fragments and demonstration pieces while on a summer teaching tour of Devon and Cornwall in the south-west of England. The piece is made of vintage textile scraps, drawings, prints, kantha-stitched remnants and a layer of laminated tissue paper (coated in a 50/50 mixture of PVA glue and water), all overstitched with my signature Bernina finishing stitch. It is backed with textile and folds neatly back into its original shape. In exhibition, the artwork hangs in folds that emphasize its original format and these can make the viewer stop and look for details.

Anne Kelly, *Devon Map*, mixed-media paper and textile.

Making Artwork Using Maps

Maps, especially vintage ones, are great for making folding booklets and other pieces of artwork. Some have a scrim or fabric backing and are ready for stitching, and I like to look out for these in second-hand bookshops and charity shops. These steps describe using a map to make a folding booklet, but you can also use this technique to laminate maps in sheets, as I have done in *Devon Map*.

1. First choose your map – you can often find one of a locality or region that you live in or near, which will have an extra resonance – then cut it along the folding lines to create a good background to the size desired for your booklet.

2. Find small pieces of thin textile or paper to suit your theme. Place these on your background using a glue stick. Try to cover at least half of the background but leave gaps to show the map off to advantage.

3. Stitch (by hand or machine) your textile and paper pieces onto the surface using simple running or straight stitch. The background can be embellished using seed stitching or kantha stitching, or with a decorative stitch on your machine.

4. Fold the booklet along natural gaps in the piece and stitch the folds down using running or straight stitch.

5. You can now back the booklet with coated paper or fabric, as desired, and add a ribbon or tie to complete it.

Amanda House: Wanderlust

Amanda House is a textile artist based in the south-west of England who makes beautiful sketchbooks using maps of her environs and her unique interpretation of them. She describes the making of one of her pieces, *Wanderlust*, here:

> 'I can spend hours poring over old maps. On finding some old road maps, I was very excited that one was of my own home county. It sat on my desk for quite some time as I looked at it, until I noticed that the folds and creases seemed to want to fall apart into book signatures.'

> 'As I gently pulled the map apart, I refolded it to see how it would fit together. I put sticky notes on each page to mark which pieces would make good signature pages and which would be back to back together (old maps are blank on the reverse, unlike modern ones). I used some really old threads I had been given to stitch the main roads and railways; it seemed more fitting than modern thread. Once all the stitching was complete, I glued the pairings together, put them into signatures and hand-stitched them to a spine of heavy watercolour paper. The excess spine paper I sandwiched between the original covers of the map, and finally added the stamped phrases to the pages.'

'I can now thumb through my little book and see how Dorset has changed over 50 years, which just makes me want to get out there and explore.'

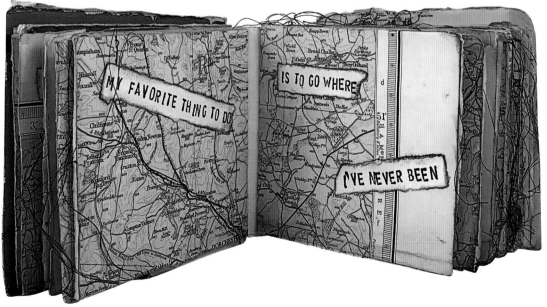

Above: Amanda House, *Wanderlust*, folding book, mixed-media textile.

Left: Amanda House, *Wanderlust*, folding book, mixed-media textile.

Travel Sewing Kits and Haberdashery

Often hotels will provide visitors with small sewing kits as part of their guest allocation. It always fascinates me to see how much can be fitted onto a folded piece of card not much larger than a matchbook. It is easy to make your own small sewing kit for travelling, like a larger version of a needlecase, using any strong material or a double layer of folded fabric. On the inside, you can leave a space for attaching a selection of needles, some embroidery threads and a small pair of scissors (airlines all have varying requirements for acceptable sizes, so check before you travel). I like to combine this into a larger zipped bag. You can see further ideas for working in cloth in the 'Resources for Journeys' section at the end of the book.

Above: Anne Kelly, *Time Together*, folding book, mixed-media textile.

Left: Anne Kelly, *Travel Kits Box Collage*, mixed media.

Chapter 2

Heading South

'Wherever you go, there you are.'

Mark Vanhoenacker,
Belgian-American pilot and author

Anne Kelly, *Southern
Inspiration Mood
Board*, mixed-media
collage.

Southern Adventures

There is something magical about leaving a cold, wet and dismal day behind, getting on a plane and re-emerging into heat, colour, new sounds and smells. The pace of life is different in warmer climates and the traces of their civilizations are often preserved in the dry heat. Peru has an amazing and complex tradition of textiles, which are some of the oldest and most influential that we can still see today. Weaving, dyeing, stitching and lacemaking are protected from as long ago as 8000 BC. Their simplicity and life-affirming humour are still striking when viewed today.

India is a textile lover's dream. It is not so much one culture as many traditions bound together by their distinctive use of colour, natural materials and narratives. In Kolkata you can see kantha work from 400 years ago that looks as if it was done yesterday. I have been fortunate to learn from craftspeople who share their techniques and processes with Western visitors.

My work in the Antipodes, which I touched on in *Textile Folk Art*, has inspired me to learn more about the history of the voyages and journeys that their native peoples made throughout the region. From the incredible sea voyages that ancestral settlers undertook to New Zealand, to the 'Songlines' of indigenous Australians, these nations are marked with signs and symbols mapping their lives, natural surroundings and travels.

The Chinese also have a long tradition of embedding signs and symbols in their works of art and literature. The placement of certain natural objects determines the meaning and function of these works and challenges the viewer to become aware of the artist's intentions. By studying the care and attention with which these are placed in the work, we can make a connection with them, many years later.

I was fortunate to have a three-week residency in Italy, in the mountains of Abruzzo. The work I produced there tells stories about the history and community of the region, including a folding book about a tailor and his trade. It was a pleasure to inhabit the mountainous and winding roads, observing the architecture and making work from it.

Anne Kelly, *Paracas Case*, mixed-media textile on cardboard case.

Southern colours, textures and scents

» *Warm, hot colours*

» *Sky and water blues*

» *Spice*

» *Floral scent*

» *Cactus*

» *Palm*

» *Insects*

» *Birds*

» *Adobe*

» *Stucco*

» *Desert*

» *Linen*

» *Cotton*

Anne Kelly, *Corali*, mixed-media textile.

Peruvian Journey

I was privileged to visit the Museo Amano in Lima, Peru, which has a large collection of pre-Colombian artefacts abandoned by tomb raiders. I was particularly impressed with the Paracas textiles, which date from 200–300 BC, made by South American people over a thousand years before the rise of the Inca. They are brightly coloured and the subjects of these images are supernatural creatures or shamans. Used as shrouds, they were intended to represent being carried to the next world by spirits. (There are also examples of these in the British Museum in London.) What is striking about them is the detail, colour and generally lively quality of the figures. They feel fresh and characterful, and when one stops to consider the amount of work involved in dyeing, spinning and weaving the textiles, it is truly impressive.

I was invited to speak at the Fashion and Textile Museum in London in July 2019 for their 'Weavers of the Clouds' exhibition, which was about the textiles of Peru. To accompany some work that I displayed at my talk, I wanted to make a piece inspired by my visit to Peru.

Anne Kelly, Paracas Case (detail of interior), mixed-media textile on cardboard case.

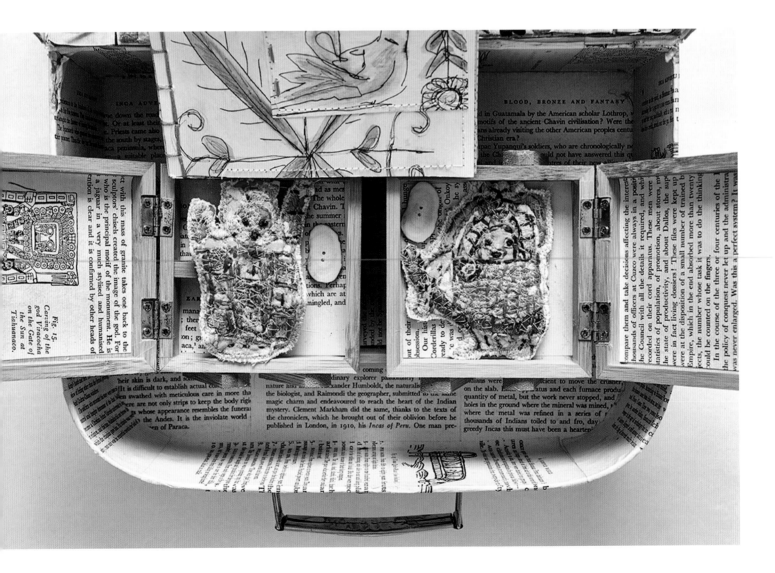

Anne Kelly, *Paracas Case* (lid detail), mixed-media textile on cardboard case.

I found the case in a charity shop and covered it with book pages from an old bookshop find (*Inca Adventure*). I used the cover of the book to line the inside of the case, as well as small samples of fabric and lace. I put together pages of my sketchbook to make a small folding book, which was then attached to the inside of the case.

I used a wooden sewing box to create a vitrine for my collection of small, Paracas-inspired soft figures, which were made from the drawings and photos that I had collected during my visit to the museum. This was also lined with book pages and trimmed with remnants of vintage ribbon, which was also added to the case, inside and out.

Making the figures, I started with blank pieces of linen and canvas, which I drew onto using fabric pens. The outlines of the figures complete, I hand-stitched in the details of the faces, bodies and armour, using my sketches and photos as reference. These were then backed with chamois leather and stuffed with wadding. Finally, they were attached to the box with string.

Nilima Sheikh: Hunarmand

I first saw Nilima Sheikh's large, free-hanging canvas pieces at the Art Institute of Chicago. She uses casein tempera paint, which simultaneously colours and stains the surface, resulting in a subtle and multi-layered effect. Born in Delhi, Nilima joins stories about her life and the history of Kashmir with information containing references to different times and geographies. This history is one of conflict and Nilima has chosen to focus on the Silk Road and journeys, using texts and images from the region. Nilima says:

'I got to know the land [of Kashmir] as a young person by walking. We used to go on treks across the valley and its mountains, often off the beaten track. At that time, the notion of trekking in the mountains for pleasure and discovery was not common, but we had friends who could guide us in the right direction, so we did it every summer. My mother was very interested in botany; she was a naturalist in many ways. This experience of seeing a world into which we could walk and discover became my first guide in my search for pictorial visualization. The land became a frequent starting point for my work.'

Hunarmand is painted on both sides. One side shows the images of craftspeople working and the other side is based on a 19th-century embroidered map shawl of the city of Srinagar.

Left: Nilima Sheikh, *Hunarmand* (figurative side), mixed-media textile on canvas.

Right: Nilima Sheikh, *Hunarmand* (map side), mixed-media textile on canvas.

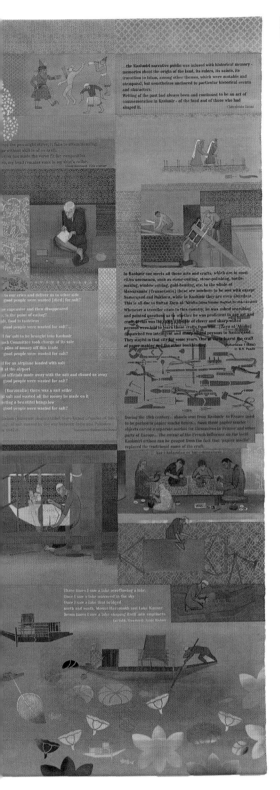

And all along flows the Jhelum,the Hydaspes, the Vyeth, the Vitasta. Through its many names never missing a spire, not a shrine or temple ghat. It touches everything and blesses everything. It connects everything, in space, in history and in spirit.

And now the Jhelum is red

Making a Stencil City

Using the work of Nilima Sheikh as a starting point, I thought it might be good to try making a piece using stencils to create a cityscape. You could use any buildings that have interesting shapes as templates to make the stencils. A good place to start is by tracing photos and simplifying the outlines.

1 Looking at the shapes and outlines of your chosen city as inspiration, draw a series of three to four stencils. You can make a variety of silhouette stencils including linear ones to create variety.

2 Arrange your stencils, starting with the larger and more linear ones first. Overlap the smaller ones as shown in the diagram to create a layered effect and shadows. Using the sponging stencil method (see Making an Indian Block Print, overleaf), apply a thin coat of acrylic, fabric or tempera paint in a range of colours to suit your theme.

3 Cut some geometric shapes from the extra fabric that you have selected. Place them in and around your stencilled prints and pin them down. Using running stitch or kantha, stitch around the pieces of fabric and into the stencilled prints. You can also add details like windows, doors and other architectural features at this stage.

Anne Kelly, *Stencilled City* – stencils, cut paper and textile printing ink.

Anne Kelly, *Stencilled City*, textile printing ink on canvas.

Linda Bassett: Threads of Identity

This garment, embellished with a map of India, drawing and writing, embodies English textile collector Linda Bassett's love affair with the subcontinent. She tells us the story of how it was made:

'When I went to Gujarat in 2016, there was one thing that I was keen to find – a Rabari shepherd's smock or *kediyun*. Despite searching markets and even stopping a camel train, one of these beautifully gathered garments could not be found. Our guide suggested the market in Bhuj, and I indeed found a battered one that was ideal for pattern-drafting.'

'At the back of Eiluned Edwards' book *Textiles and Dress of Gujarat*, there are diagrams of some of the garments held in the V&A's collection. One is a Rabari kediyun. I used my antique one and the measurements from his book to make a pattern. The first kediyun I made was blue and I used some khadi cotton from Gujarat. I embroidered it with kantha stitching and block-printed elephants on the yoke. The concept of the *Threads of My Identity* had resonated with me for a while, the strands that make me who I am. I decided to stitch a mind map of them onto a white linen kediyun, alongside a map of my beloved India.'

'I often leave the threads at the end of my work. I like the suggestion of being unfinished, much like our journey through life. And so developed a *Kediyun of Identity*, stitched with thoughts and memories of what makes me who I am.'

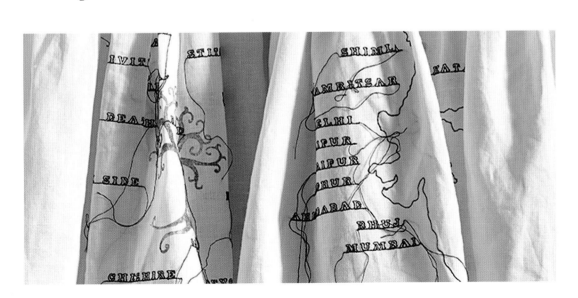

Above: Linda Bassett, *My Kediyun*, handmade linen garment with machine embroidery and block printing.

Left: Linda Bassett, *My Kediyun* (detail), handmade linen garment with machine embroidery and block printing.

Maharini Gardens

I was lucky enough to visit Jaipur in Rajasthan on a teaching tour, to work on block printing and a project based on the local gardens. Gardens in India are more architectural than plant-based, as is common in Britain. The shape of the planted beds, the garden buildings, paintings and decoration on the walls are all hugely inspiring and provided a background for the collages that we made while in the city. Jaipur is a city surrounded by walls – the arches and details on and around the walls add character to the landscape. The collages were started during our stay in the city and assembled using a mixture of block printing, fabric cut-outs and hand stitch.

Above: Jaipur cityscape.

Left: Anne Kelly, *Maharini Gardens*, mixed-media textile.

Making a Garden Collage

There are so many elements of this project that are exciting and easily available. You can use wooden printing blocks, rubber stamps, vintage textiles and fragments of embroidery to complete your piece. Look to real gardens and photos of them for inspiration – different cultures interpret them in unique and artistic ways.

1 Use a range of wooden printing blocks and rubber stamps with a garden theme to create a range of prints. Use the simple sponge and acrylic paint method (see Making an Indian Block Print, overleaf) using plant colours – greens, yellows and reds. When they are dry, cut around them leaving a 5mm (¼in) border.

2 Choose a neutral background, possibly an old vintage fabric or strong material like calico, linen union or light canvas, cut no bigger than around 30cm (12in) square. Cut out scraps of fabric that suit the theme and overlap them with the block prints to create an interesting background. When happy with their position, lightly glue them into place using a glue stick.

3 When all the background pieces are in position you can use tacking (basting) stitches to attach them to the fabric. If you use interesting and uniform stitching then the tacking can become a part of the design. The piece will look better and more dimensional as you continue to add stitch to it.

To embellish the piece, add hand embroidery and small pieces of ribbon, buttons and machine embroidery if desired. The finished work can be mounted onto another piece of fabric or wrapped around a canvas. I mounted mine onto a bag and covered the reverse side in plain fabric.

Above: Jaipur market shop.

Left: Anne Kelly, Indian fabric Inspiration board.

Making an Indian Block Print

I chose some small printing blocks which are very useful for making plants and trees on fabric. They are even more versatile when you consider, or 'audition', as they say in New Zealand, the background fabric or colour. Often the reverse side of the textile can be more useful than the front. The colour of the printing ink or fabric paint that you use has to contrast with the fabric. The interplay of the pattern and textile is striking and can be very effective when sewn into a larger piece.

1 Apply the paint or printing ink to your chosen block with a small sponge, dabbing not smearing.

2 Lay a padded or spongy surface underneath the fabric you are printing onto – when choosing fabric, avoid anything heavily textured or stretchy – then press the block onto the fabric.

3 Consider the contrast between your base colour and paint. Repeat to layer colour and pattern as you choose.

New Zealand Boat Folder

New Zealand is a mix of cultures and heritage from all over the region and the world. The sea is omnipresent and binds together the stories from North and South Island. A visitor from the West feels at home but also notices new types of flora and fauna, a different landscape at every turn.

Inspired by the 2018 exhibition 'Oceania' at the Royal Academy of Arts, London, and an example of a Maori carved wooden boat that I saw at the Museum of New Zealand Te Papa Tongarewa, Wellington, I made this piece using a pen-holder folder and some images of these types of boats. I used a drawing of boats to line the folder with and covered it with pieces of an embroidered sampler.

Anne Kelly, *New Zealand Boat Folder*, mixed-media textile.

New Zealand Map

My map of New Zealand was a gift from a student when I was teaching in West Sussex, who in turn had been given it by a New Zealand visitor. It was a vintage map and made from strong paper. I backed it with old cotton sheeting on one side and tissue paper on the other, coating it with a 50/50 mixture of PVA glue and water. I added pieces of fabric gifted to me by students and a set of travel tags that I had been given by my group at Fibre Arts New Zealand. I used my overstitching technique to cover the map and soften the fabric. When teaching in New Zealand I was also given a Maori *kete* (basket), which I decided to use to store the map in.

Anne Kelly, *New Zealand Map and Kete*, mixed-media textile on paper.

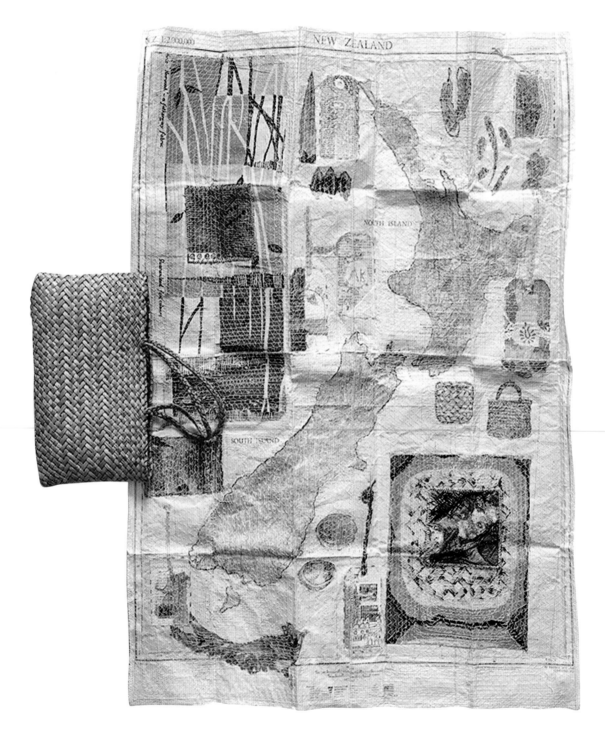

Australian Birds Tea Towels

On my first visit to Australia I was astounded by the colourful birds I saw everywhere. I noticed that there were also many bird- and nature-themed tea towels available in the charity or 'opportunity' shops. On my most recent visit I decided to collect several of these tea towels to create an 'Australian Rainforest' piece.

For inspiration I visited the amazing Sea Acres Rainforest boardwalk in Port Macquarie, New South Wales. The patterns on the trees and the shapes of the leaves were striking and can be seen in examples of indigenous art. I wanted to create a monumental piece for my solo exhibition, 'Anne Kelly – Well Travelled', at the Ruthin Craft Centre, North Wales, in spring 2021. I made a large drawing of the plants and birds that I wanted to use on the piece. I transferred them onto the reverse side of the tea towels and then 'drew' the outline on. Then I went around the outlines with a dark free-motion stitch. I then worked on the top side of the pieces with my overstitching technique with the addition of some colour.

Above: Rosella, New South Wales, Australia.

Left: Anne Kelly, *Australian Birds Tea Towels*, mixed-media textile.

Articles of Ancestry

I was invited to exhibit at the Timeless Textiles Gallery in Newcastle, Australia, after my last visit in 2016. It is the only commercial textiles gallery in Australia and has a long tradition of introducing emerging and established artists from Australia and abroad to a new audience. I wanted my exhibition 'Articles of Ancestry' to connect to the themes of travel and migration that I had started to explore in my 2018 book, *Textile Folk Art*.

The exhibition space ran to two rooms and I had a variety of work on show, including my '12 Dresses' collection, which is about the women in my father's family. I made a feature of the *Home Fires Dress*, made from French *brocante*, which was used on the exhibition poster and hung over the fireplace in the gallery.

I also showed a new artwork, *Family Portraits*. For this piece, I used a combination of Chinese textiles, treated paper, ribbon and lace. I decided to work from photographs of my family at different stages of their lives. I used a free-motion outline and painted in elements of the skin tone to create a more solid shape.

Above: Anne Kelly, *Family Portraits*, mixed-media textiles, *in situ* at Timeless Textiles Gallery, Newcastle, Australia

Left: Anne Kelly, *Home Fires Dress*, mixed-media textile.

Eastern Embroideries and Beijing Reader

In my practice I often write and give talks about my work and influences. Last year I was speaking to a guild in south London whose members gave me a textile book from the beginning of the 20th century called *Eastern Embroideries*. 'You can do something with this!' they said.

I wanted to combine my stitching with the stitching in the sample book. I took it apart so that each double page became a block. I added scenes from a vintage tourist book on 'Old Peking', which were then hand-stitched into the background. I then applied my characteristic overstitch to the whole piece, which had the effect of flattening the additions and making it more cohesive.

Right: Anne Kelly, *Eastern Embroideries*, mixed-media and embroidery linen textile.

Left: Anne Kelly, *Beijing Reader* (closed), mixed-media textile.

Another piece I have made recently on a Far Eastern theme is *Beijing Reader*, inspired by the chance find of a vintage cabinet, which I re-covered and decorated after much cleaning. As you can see from the photo, it has a decorative painted front.

On the inside I used some child's clothing and shoes found in Beijing and two folding books that I made during a recent Chinese visit. I lined the box with maps of Beijing and pages from a Chinese textile pattern book. The finished piece has been exhibited in several venues.

Anne Kelly, *Beijing Reader* (open), mixed-media textile.

An Italian Residency

In the summer of 2018, I was an artist in residence in Abruzzo, Italy, in the town of Farindola, which is near the Gran Sasso National Park. I was there for three weeks of work and exhibitions. I made some large painted collages of the area around the town, using fabrics found at the markets nearby. These included tea towels and brightly coloured tablecloths.

The author in her studio at the Farindola residency, Abruzzo, Italy.

I was given a pair of old hand-operated Singer sewing machines to work with in a cool, tiled studio. We had an open studio event where I met a retired tailor from the village in his eighties. Raffaele was apprenticed to a local tailor at the age of 12. He recalled how rural Italian tailors visited farms alongside cobblers to outfit the men (women made their own clothing). They were paid in wheat and the village used to have a fabric shop where they could buy supplies.

Studio at Farindola Residency, Abruzzo.

Inspired by his stories, I made a folding book about Raffaele. *A Farindola Fable* was made from a sketchbook I had received in China, and I replaced pages with textile and added collage. It is a simplified version and was included in our final studio display. It was wonderful to be able to work uninterrupted for such a long period and to reflect back on a lovely, vibrant community.

Above left: Anne Kelly, *A Farindola Fable* (detail), mixed media.

Above right: Anne Kelly, *A Farindola Fable* sketchbook, mixed media.

Chapter 3

Due North

'One can't paint New York as it is,
rather as it is felt.'

Georgia O'Keeffe, American artist

Anne Kelly, *Northern
Inspiration Mood
Board*, mixed media
on board.

Headed North

Northern countries are inspirational and share a variety of textile traditions, as I explored in my book *Textile Folk Art*. In this chapter, I begin by looking at a project that means a lot to me, *100 Years Haberdashery*, which was inspired by two hearts that I made for the Embroiderers' Guild in the UK. The project expanded to include two sewing boxes and a sketchbook. Much of the work was exhibited in a two-person show at the Mississippi Valley Textile Museum in Ontario, Canada, in early 2019.

In this chapter I will also look at textile artists and makers who interact with the landscape and their surroundings in a distinctive way. Catherine Blackburn and Zachari Logan made a unique collaborative piece using contemporary drawing and traditional indigenous beading techniques. Julia Tselkova's knitted mittens are landscapes in themselves. Brooke Atherton's very personal work connects with her own patch of the North American landscape.

Maud Lewis was an inspiring folk artist from Nova Scotia and her appearance in this chapter leads us into a section on houses and their place in our travels. Houses can symbolically represent elements of our childhood and memory, as I discovered in *Textile Folk Art*. In this chapter, I am interested in how they become repositories for collections that are imbued with a sense of place. Following this, we look at carrying cases – for travel, as vitrines for display and as objects in themselves.

Anne Kelly, *A Very Big Country* (detail), mixed-media textile.

Anne Kelly, *Home Fires Dress* (detail), mixed-media textile.

Northern places and spaces

» *Cold, darker colours*

» *Snow, snowflakes*

» *Ice, icicles*

» *Conifers*

» *Log cabins*

» *Lakes*

» *Rivers*

» *Autumn leaves*

» *Knitting*

» *Wool*

» *Down*

Stitched: A Homecoming

When interpreting a place, time or event in any art form it is the artist's vision and viewpoint that we see it from. I have an affinity with northern countries as that is where I come from. As we age, we often try to reclaim our past and that of our families, expressing it in our research and our work.

Anne Kelly, *100 Years Haberdashery*, part of the 'Stitched – A Homecoming' exhibition, *in situ* at Mississippi Valley Textile Museum, Almonte, Ontario, Canada.

I was invited to exhibit as part of a two-person show at the Mississippi Valley Textile Museum near Ottawa in Canada. It's an old mill that has been renovated to create an atmospheric exhibition and workshop space. I wanted to showcase some work with Canadian roots, like my *100 Years Haberdashery* project, which remembers, celebrates and honours my grandmother and her family members during the First World War.

Anne Kelly, 'Stitched – A Homecoming' exhibition, *in situ* at Mississippi Valley Textile Museum, Almonte, Ontario, Canada.

Haberdashery Sewing Box

For this project, I created a sewing box in memory of my maternal grandmother, who lived in Northern Ontario. She was a great needlewoman who made all kinds of textile items, from hooked rugs and quilts to lace and crochet. There is a book laid into the base of the box, and I embellished the old sewing box with fragments of ephemera and stitched work. Although telling my grandmother's personal story, I also wanted the box to represent the lives of the women who lived in Canada in and around the time of the First World War.

Anne Kelly, *100 Years Haberdashery* (closed), mixed-media textile on wood box.

Making a Decorated Sewing Box

If you want to make a decorated sewing box, the method is similar to the *London Collar Case* project described in Chapter 1. Here's a list of things that you might need:

» A wooden box with relatively smooth surfaces

» Vintage papers – pages from old books, maps, wrapping paper

» Fabric remnants and scraps of embroidery, buttons and ribbons

» PVA glue, acrylic wax or acrylic varnish

» Glue stick

» Glue gun (optional)

» Sewing notions

» Family photographs

» An old book with an interesting spine and cover that will fit inside the box (mine came from a French junk shop)

Anne Kelly, *100 Years Haberdashery* (open), mixed-media textile on wood box.

War Stories Hearts

I was inspired to make work after finding a cache of photographs when looking through my family archive. They showed some members of my grandmother's family, enjoying a day out in the countryside in Northern Ontario, with several of the men in uniform on leave. I found this very poignant as they must have seen some horrific things during their time in Europe. There was a particularly moving image of these soldiers around a cloth-covered table entitled 'Northern Ontario Men in France, 1918'. This picture became the focal point for a heart I made for the '100 Hearts War Stories' project, devised by the Embroiderers' Guild, UK, to commemorate the 100th anniversary of the end of the First World War. I used a fabric transfer and hand-coloured photograph of the men with elements of collage and ephemera surrounding the piece, including a vintage tape measure as a trim.

Anne Kelly, *Heart*, mixed-media textile, made for the Embroiderers' Guild '100 Hearts War Stories' project, *in situ* at Norwich Cathedral, Norfolk, UK.

I made a companion piece for the original heart for the 'Stitched – A Homecoming' exhibition in Ontario, Canada. This heart was more about the domestic scene at the time and featured a woman working at home on its front side.

Anne Kelly, *Canadian Home Heart*, mixed-media textile.

56

Blue Book

The original heart toured from Alexandra Palace in north London to Norwich Cathedral in East Anglia as part of the group exhibition '100 Hearts War Stories', and I documented my visit to see it in a sketchbook, *Blue Book*. I used pages from an old ledger found at my grandmother's farm as background pages. Then I drew stages of the journey in sketch form, adding collaged ephemera and colour when I returned to the studio.

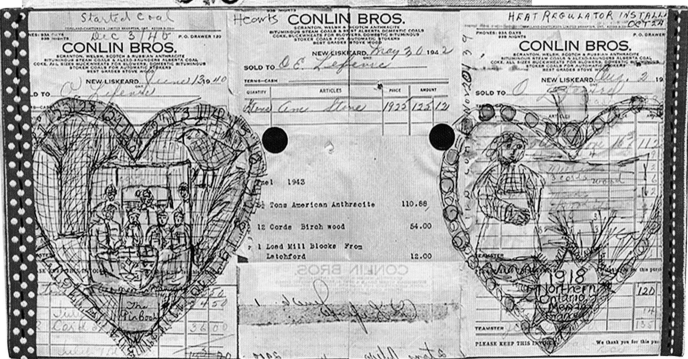

Anne Kelly, *Blue Book*
sketchbook and case,
textile and paper.

Catherine Blackburn and Zachari Logan: Ditch Flowers

Catherine Blackburn and Zachari Logan are Canadian artists working respectively in the disciplines of beaded jewellery and fine art. They worked collaboratively to create *Inherently Stitched (Ditch Flowers)*, a piece that is influenced by First Nation beading techniques and Catherine's heritage but which has an altogether modern approach and meaning, as she describes here:

> 'I wanted this wearable piece of art to break free of gender conformity in its design. I wanted to incorporate ideas of the business-class working "men's" suit and tie, specifically a tie … it literally dissects the shape and reconstructs [it] as a bolo necklace. The work was then infused with a cropped replica version of Zachari's delicately detailed floral drawing. The process itself was done using micro Czech seed beads utilizing the two-thread stitch technique.'

It is wonderful to see how this example of their art combines traditional Dene (First Nation) culture with a new interpretation of it to produce a unique and contemporary piece of wearable art.

Catherine Blackburn and Zachari Logan, *Inherently Stitched (Ditch Flowers)* (detail), beaded and mixed-media jewellery.

Catherine Blackburn and Zachari Logan, *Inherently Stitched (Ditch Flowers)*, beaded and mixed-media jewellery.

Julia Tselkova: Arctic Circle

I found these amazing embroidered mittens by Julia Tselkova on the social media platform Instagram. She lives in Russia and describes how this has influenced her work:

> 'I love the North and to embroider – the long winter, the cold sea, tundra and taiga.
> I am most inspired by the colours of the North. I can embroider in the same calm shades.
> A few years ago, I moved to live in the Arctic Circle and came up with the idea of knitting woollen mittens and embroidering aspects of my region [the Chukotka] on them.'

The mittens are a perfect combination of utility and decoration, and a memorable way to celebrate Julia's surroundings.

Julia Tselkova,
untitled composition,
mixed media and
textile.

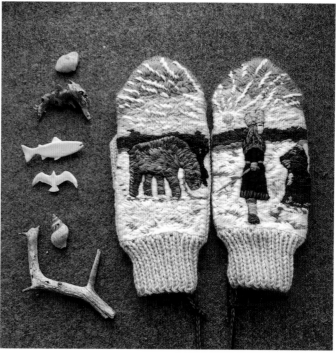

Julia Tselkova,
untitled composition,
mixed media and
textile.

A Very Big Country

I used two maps of Northern Quebec, Canada, for this project, which were attached to fabric and laminated by brushing with a 50/50 mixture of PVA glue and water. They were stencilled with silhouettes of native animals – an owl, a bird, a whale and a bear – inspired by Cape Dorset Arts. The pieces were then overstitched on the machine, with the main objects in them stitched around with backstitch. I added some contemporary embroidered patches, which represent a more current view of the country. I used rubber stamps to add place names and wooden blocks for the larger words, which were then stitched over in white.

I combined the pieces of the maps together and overlapped them slightly to create a quilt-like effect. The finished work folded up into a slipcase specially made for it. It was displayed hung from the wall with clamps with the folds left in place. These become part of the displayed piece, with shadows and rough edges adding to the texture of the work.

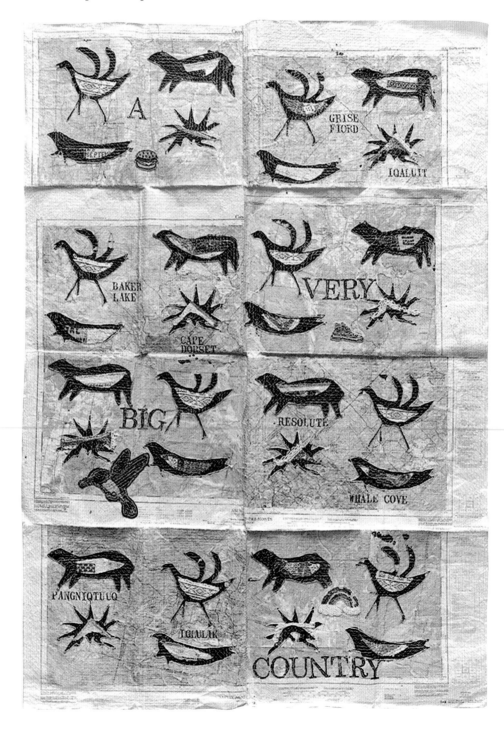

Anne Kelly, *A Very Big Country*, screen-printed map, laminated and stitched on textile.

Brooke Atherton: How to Hold an Elusive Memory

Brooke Atherton lives in the Rocky Mountains in Montana, USA, creating expansive works based on her hikes, exploring and listening to people's stories. Her pieces refer to specific events and people in her life. She evocatively describes her work:

'I am drawn to the small, intimate stories that illuminate an idea, relationship or event, while I live in a place that has been called a stage of mythic proportions. Reading about the American West and Montana does not prepare you for the reality of driving across hundreds of miles of flat, dry, empty land. Its geology surprises me over and over, jutting out of the flat, dry ground into endless, open sky.'

'I describe my work as a version of the journals left by explorers like Lewis and Clark two hundred years before me. Meandering across the landscape, I pick up small things like feathers or pieces of shale. These artefacts are added into my memory bank: textile maps, calendars and landscapes that describe a place and time. I walk these trails often and informally record changes that have occurred since the last time I was here.'

Brooke Atherton, How to Hold an Elusive Memory (detail) mixed-media textile panel.

'We are the ones who have the big fire, the one with all the children and dogs around it, so they all eventually wander over and sit with us for a while. I listen to their stories. The owls and hawks and jays fly overhead and I pick up their dropped feathers. Unknown animals walk quietly around us all night; I watch the dogs lift their heads; they move to the edges of the light and I imagine what they might be seeing or listening to.'

Brooke Atherton, How to Hold an Elusive Memory, mixed-media textile panel.

'We watch planets and stars; they change positions over the summer and then we leave when the snow comes; I take home with me more than enough ideas for another year of textile work. There is a Japanese word for a small thing that brings you suddenly, joyously back to fond memories, not with a wistful longing for what is past, but with an appreciation of the good times.'

Maud Lewis's House

I made this piece after visiting Maud Lewis's house at the Art Gallery of Nova Scotia in Halifax, Canada. Maud's life and the house in which she lived have been widely documented in print and on film but nothing prepares you for the fresh and colourful decorations she painted on her house and in her artwork. The entire house has been reconstructed after being moved from its original location to a bespoke space in the art gallery. Maud's paintings tell stories about her life and where she lived in rural Nova Scotia. The flora and fauna she saw cover all the surfaces.

Maud Lewis's House,
in situ at Art Gallery
of Nova Scotia, Halifax,
Canada.

Maudie's House

I wanted to pay homage to Maud's vision using an embroidered tablecloth as a base. I drew the outline of the house using fabric pens and vintage Indian printing blocks to create a pattern on the side and roof of the house. I then drew and hand-stitched motifs based on her designs onto the door and windows. The piece was then overstitched and backed. It was first exhibited in the UK at my 'Folk House' exhibition at Compton Verney in Warwickshire, and later at the Knitting and Stitching Shows in London and Harrogate as part of the Embroiderers' Guild members' exhibition, 'Home'.

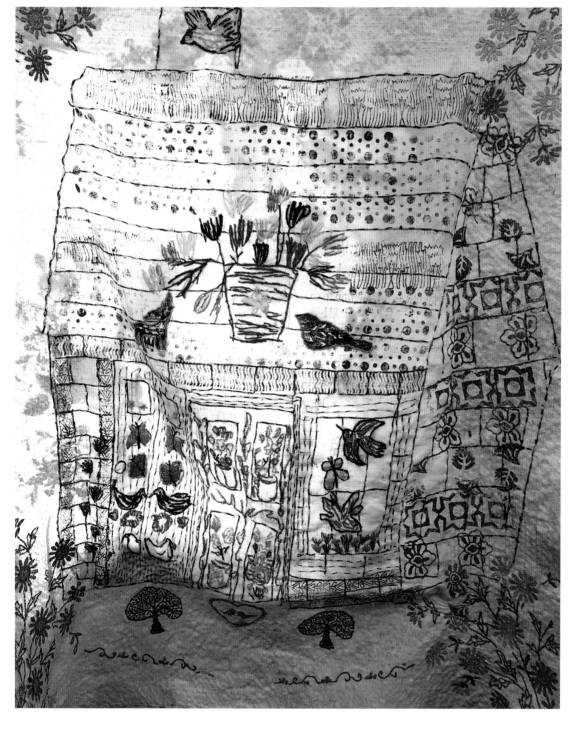

Anne Kelly, *Maudie's House*, mixed-media textile.

Houses at Compton Verney

I was invited to be guest artist at Compton Verney, where the British Folk Art collection is based, during their annual Textile Fair. I was given a large ground-floor room, which I was able to arrange for exhibition. I placed two ladders side by side and put a rope between them to suspend some of my pieces featuring houses and buildings from my Farindola residency in Abruzzo, Italy (see Chapter 2).

Anne Kelly, 'Folk House' exhibition *in situ* at Compton Verney, Warwickshire, UK.

Tudor House

Following on from my first doll's house, which I included in my book *Textile Folk Art*, I decided to create two more pieces based on charity shop finds I had at home. The first of these, the *Tudor House*, was a large and very heavy wooden construction, decorated and embellished with pieces from a map of Dorset and a Welsh tea towel, and lined with pages from a vintage children's science book. I used some blocks from a wooden toy set to enhance its architectural details.

Above: Anne Kelly, *Tudor House* (closed), mixed-media textile on wood.

Left: Anne Kelly, *Tudor House* (open), mixed-media textile on wood.

Stamp House

My *Stamp House* doll's house was a vehicle for finally using my childhood stamp collection to decorate the shingle roof. A pair of 1960s tea towels provided much of the textile decoration, which also includes snippets of hand embroidery and ribbon. The house is lined with book pages as well as some weaving samples which I found inside the house when I bought it. This piece will form part of my forthcoming exhibition at the Ruthin Craft Centre, North Wales.

Above: Anne Kelly, *Stamp House* (side view), mixed-media textile on wood.

Left: Anne Kelly, *Stamp House*, mixed-media textile on wood.

Rigg Doll's House, Tunbridge Wells Museum

One of the most popular items in the collection of the Tunbridge Wells Museum in Kent is a large 19th-century doll's house, which measures 1.8 x 1.4m (6 x 4½ft). The house was made during the 1840s in the UK for two small girls, near to where their family were living – a gift from their father who was a London stockbroker. There was a fashion for doll's houses at that time and the size of this one was intended to display the family's wealth and standing in the community. When the family moved to Argentina, the house went with them.

Riggs Doll's House, *in situ* at Tunbridge Wells Museum, Kent.

When Mary Searle, one of the sisters, died in the 1930s, her housekeeper passed the house on to the eldest of Mary's adopted sons, Dr Rigg, who was now living in Southborough, near Tunbridge Wells, and so this well-travelled house returned home to the UK. The 'Rigg Doll's House' stayed with the doctor's family until 1957 when it joined the museum. Collectors and experts who have examined the doll's house and its contents have observed that the furniture in it must have been specially made for the house by skilled craftsmen. If you want to see the doll's house for yourself, the museum is currently closed but it will open again in 2021/2022 renamed The Amelia at the Amelia Scott, as part of a revitalized learning hub.

Dresses with Meaning

As with houses, children's dresses and other garments can be imbued with memory and stories. They can represent places, journeys and travel. I collect vintage clothing and like to incorporate them into larger pieces like the *Hudson River Valley Dress*. This piece reminds me of colonial times in New England. I recently visited the amazing Warm Brook Barn in Arlington, Vermont, a location that embodies the sense of place that this dress evokes. I was tutoring there for French General – it is a haven of peace and creativity.

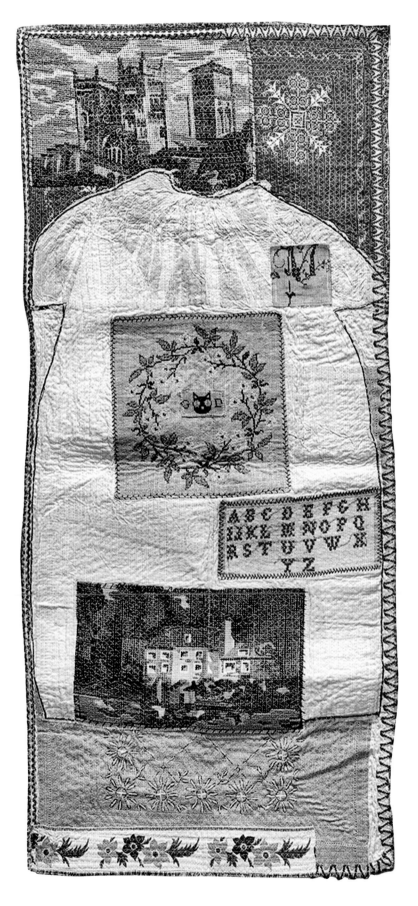

Above: Anne Kelly, *Hudson River Valley Dress* (detail), mixed-media textile.

Right: Anne Kelly, *Hudson River Valley Dress*, mixed-media textile.

Tree of Life Case

I like working with suitcases and travel cases, covering them with stitched panels and decorative pieces of *brocante* and trim. This piece was made from an embroidery started in Italy and finished in my studio, using a popular 'Tree of Life' motif referenced in my book *Textile Folk Art*.

Anne Kelly, *Tree of Life Case*, mixed-media textile on suitcase.

Haberdashery Cases

I found some small cardboard and metal cases in a charity shop and decided to use them to showcase two pieces of archive embroidery that were made about 15 years ago and included in my book *Textile Nature*. I wanted to combine articles of haberdashery and natural history book pages in the pieces. I began by covering each case with book pages inside and out, pasted with a glue stick and laminated with an acrylic varnish. Then I chose the objects to go inside each case. This was done by size and suitability of the subject matter.

For mounting the embroideries, I glued some vintage wooden cotton reels to the base of the main portion of the cases. The embroidered works were attached to these with the addition of a piece of cloth, glued to the reels and stitched to the originals. For inside the lid of the cases, I used a vintage book cover for the smaller case and more haberdashery items (cotton reels, tape measures, needle packets) on the other. I completed the cases by adding ribbon around the edges and applying another couple of coats of acrylic varnish, inside and out.

These pieces were exhibited in the inaugural Society of Embroidered Works (SEW) exhibition at the Clerkenwell Gallery in London.

Anne Kelly,
Haberdashery Case
'Violet', mixed media.

Anne Kelly,
Haberdashery Case
'Bay', mixed media.

Chapter 4

Stopping Places

*'repaired with light
and fresh air
homeward bound'*

Sarah Salway,
British novelist and poet

Anne Kelly, *Peacock
Jacket*, mixed-media
textile.

Travel Tags

We are literally stopping here, looking at the places and landscapes that inspire us. As part of my gallery at the Knitting and Stitching Shows in the UK in 2018/2019, I made some covered suitcases and asked for travel tags, and an amazing array came my way from 150 contributors. I made a sign for the exhibition to commemorate the incredible response.

Returning home after a time away can give you a new perspective on your home and surroundings. In this chapter, we will be looking at locations that are close to our heart and ways of expressing our connections with them. Travel can be local, and one could argue that focusing on your immediate environment gives you a more meaningful understanding of it. Here we look at the work of several artists and makers who share that personal relationship with their surroundings, expressing and telling stories about them at the same time.

Anne Kelly, garden finds from the author's garden.

The language of home

Anne Kelly, *Travel Tags Sign*, mixed-media textile.

Julian Rowe: Artist Books

I first saw Julian Rowe's work when I exhibited with him many years ago at the 'Made by Hand' craft exhibition at Kent County Hall in Maidstone in the south-east of England. I was curious about his journeys and his portrayal of the Kent countryside, where I too have made my home. I admire his use of mixed media and collage to create these two lovely book forms. Julian shares his thoughts on his process:

'My creative adventure as a whole has followed a long path from an exploration of abstraction founded in the shapes and forms of the landscape, to an interest in narrative and history and their relationship to place. I think this was an inevitable development, as there is such a close connection at a fundamental level between making a journey and telling a story … these two basic human experiences are intimately bound together.'

'The diverse group of artist books I made between 1996 and 2004 reflect this transition in my work, as the book form is essentially a narrative one. They are all based on my explorations of places that are local to me, but some at least contain references to a wider world, and all of them acknowledge human interventions in the landscape.'

Julian Rowe, *Eden Bridges* (above) and *Nineveh* (below) artist books, mixed media on paper.

Kent Maps

Inspired by a charity shop find of local maps, I decided to make two different folding books. The first is a small concertina book form, using maps of towns in Kent. I free-machined tree motifs over the top and added colourful lines to emphasize the outlines of the maps.

Anne Kelly, *Kent Map Sketchbook* with case, mixed-media paper and textile.

I also made a larger map book, with pages stitched together to create a bound edge. I added some found insect embroideries superimposed over the pages. Finally, I made a case for the piece using a remnant from an unfinished tapestry found in a charity shop.

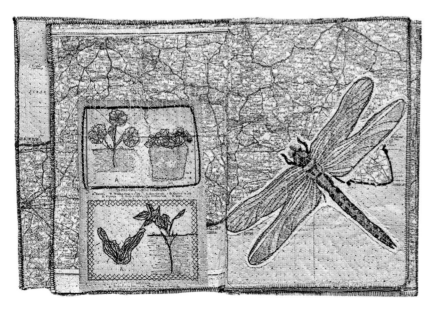

Above left: Anne Kelly, *Bee Sketchbook* (closed), mixed media on paper.

Left: Anne Kelly, *Bee Sketchbook* (open) with case, mixed media on paper.

Travelling Sketchbooks

I always like to have a folding book at hand to stitch on, when travelling near or far. They are portable and easy to pick up when you have a few minutes free. I make mine with a combination of textile and paper, which is laminated and stitched together using the process described in Chapter 1. I am always pleased to look back on them as they are a concrete memory of an adventure.

There are further suggestions and instructions for working in paper in the 'Resources for Journeys' section at the end of this book.

Ali Ferguson: To the Creel

I enjoyed teaching with Scottish textile artist Ali Ferguson in New Zealand and to observe at close quarters the intense preparation and examination of her subject matter. We both share a fondness for vintage textiles and ephemera. Ali describes herself as an artist, embroiderer and collector of stories and it is these stories that are at the heart of her textile practice.

Her project 'To the Creel' is inspired by a collection of postcards sent to the women of one East Lothian fishing family. Dated in the 1920s and postmarked all the way up the east coast of Scotland, round to Mallaig and Greenock on the west and journeying in the other direction as far south as Great Yarmouth on England's East Anglian coast, the cards were sent by the men while away at sea.

Addressed 'Dear Wife', 'Dear Sister' and 'Dear Mother', these postcards provided that vital link to home. They report on the important issues of the day – the weather, the fishing and, essentially, the money that would be brought home. While the words come from the men, the stripes in these pieces represent the women. An important part of their identity as fishwives was the blue-and-white striped skirts and aprons they wore. Text from the postcards is printed onto calico as well as being meticulously embroidered.

Some pieces include knitting needles to represent the Gansey sweaters that the men wore. Each family would design their own pattern and the story goes that these were used as a means of identification if tragedy struck and the men were lost at sea. Knitted by hand, they provided another link between voyager and home.

Ali layers, hand stitches and pins her materials together, and in doing so imagines piecing together these little fragments of everyday life. Displayed in museum-style cases, these artworks, she believes, offer a tiny glimpse into lives all but forgotten or overlooked, an homage to the memory of a way of life that has all but disappeared.

Above: Anne Kelly, *A Snowy Adventure*. mixed-media textile folding piece.

Left: Ali Ferguson, *Dear Sister*, mixed-media textile in shadow box.

Below: Ali Ferguson, *Dear Wife*, mixed-media textile in shadow box.

Western Weeds Sketchbook

In the summer of 2019, I went on a three-week teaching tour of the UK's West Country and made a sketchbook to keep while I was travelling. I wanted to capture a small aspect of each place I visited and to record the plant life I was seeing by the roads and paths. It was a good way to engage with a project after some long and tiring working days.

I made the book using pages from an old natural history book of the area, covering the fronts with unbleached muslin and the backs with tissue paper.

I drew the 'weeds' with a fine-line pen, colouring them in with watercolour crayons. They were then stitched into by hand, and the date and place recorded.

Above: Anne Kelly,
*Western Weeds
Sketchbook* (open),
mixed media on paper.

Left: Anne Kelly,
*Western Weeds
Sketchbook* (cover),
mixed media on paper.

Debbie Lyddon: Moments of Being

I exhibited next to British textile artist Debbie Lyddon at the 2016 Knitting and Stitching Show in London. It was instructive to see the attention to detail and meticulous documentation she puts into her practice, as she describes here:

'The pattern of my everyday life is defined by the season. In the short days of winter, I walk, as the dim light allows, wrapped up in a hat and gloves as protection from the bitterly cold easterly wind. In summer, everything is bounded by the state of the tide and I'm often to be found on a boat. This routine of walking and sailing the edge of the land and the sea and the marshes at Wells-next-the-Sea, Norfolk is the foundation of all my work.'

'"Moments of Being" is inspired by a series of vividly remembered encounters and engagements with this landscape. Each work notates the memory of an event or observation: the sun moving over the marsh and creating shadows, the clink of halyards knocking against masts, the shape of a bend in the creek or the way saltwater marks my clothes. These are not unusual experiences but are personal and intensely remembered moments.'

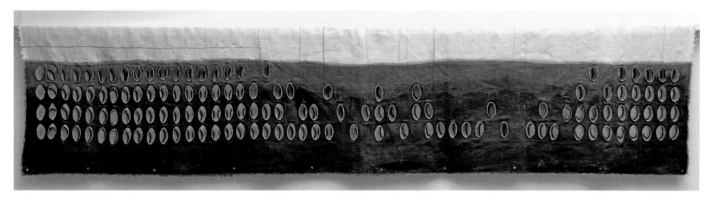

Above: Debbie Lyddon, *Sluice Creek Cloths Masts and Halyards*, mixed-media textile.

Left: Debbie Lyddon, *Sluice Creek Cloths Masts and Halyards* (detail), mixed-media textile.

Archana Pathak: Transient Boundaries

As well as observing external borders, artists constantly examine the internal motivation and memories associated with place. Archana Pathak uses her identity as the map of her work, which although abstract is relatable and moving. She explains:

> 'The question of belonging has found crafty ways to stay at the centre of my life – be it when as a child, every few years, I moved from city to city with my parents, or when I chose London as a new home leaving an unclaimed heap of years behind in India. Through my practice, I am exploring the interplay between memory, place and identity, and working with found memory ephemera such as old photographs, postcards, letters, diaries and maps.'

> 'Often these artefacts are old maps that bring forth the evolving nature of boundaries – both physical as well as psychological. Along with these constantly evolving boundaries are the identities that are being reshaped. I use bare-minimum tools and use stitch to recreate a sense of belonging that helps me stay connected with what is fading but precious in life.'

Archana Pathak,
Borders (detail),
mixed-media textile.

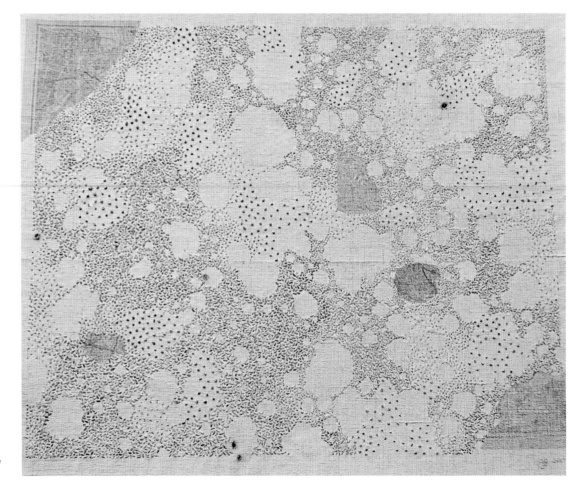

Archana Pathak,
Transient Boundaries,
mixed-media textile.

Sophie's Passport

I realized last year that it had been 70 years since my paternal grandmother and her family fled Nazi Germany for the UK. I found a copy of the passport that she used to leave the country. I used a fabric transfer as a base and embellished with lace and fragments of textile before adding a fabric backing to it (a similar technique to the map lamination method described in Chapter 1). The piece was exhibited in my 'Articles of Ancestry' solo show in the Timeless Textiles Gallery in Newcastle, Australia, and sold to a collector there.

Anne Kelly, *Sophie's Passport*, mixed-media textile.

Anne Kelly, *Sophie's Passport* (detail), mixed-media textile.

Livia Papiernik: Wear Your Heritage with Pride

Livia Papiernik is a textile artist whose work exhibits a strong graphic and a colourful signature. She graduated from London's Royal School of Needlework in 2018, where she studied traditional hand embroidery. Livia now works as a freelance embroidery artist, working on commissions, artworks and her jewellery line.

Livia's love for textiles and embroidery comes primarily from a desire for story-telling, as she explains: 'The historical context associated with textiles fuels my creative work and creates an energy that I embrace to narrate my own personal or historical stories.' The collection 'Wear Your Heritage with Pride' grew from Livia questioning her own roots and identity. Saddened by the new rise in xenophobia and narrow-minded views on immigration, she challenged these ideas while ultimately questioning what classifies someone as an immigrant. Having grown up in a society with an ever-widening racial, religious and cultural diversity, Livia has always embraced the richness that it can bring.

Exploring her ancestry and heritage, Livia follows her French roots all the way back to Poland before the Jews were persecuted during the Holocaust. She also explores her English side to the East End of London and back to Ireland, Scotland and central Europe, where many of her family come from.

Livia uses goldwork and silk-shading techniques alongside unconventional materials, bold colours and 3D embellishment. Whitework and lace are predominant inspirations for her surface designs and these intertwine with her graphic family portraits to create a unique family tree that explores personal and global issues of identity. By embroidering her artwork onto a garment, she reflects how our heritage is part of us and how we carry it with us everywhere.

Above right: Livia Papiernik, 'Wear Your Heritage with Pride' collection, embroidered textile garment (detail).

Right: Livia Papiernik, 'Wear Your Heritage with Pride' collection, embroidered textile garment (detail).

Self-Portrait

I was given an embroidered piece of linen that looked like me as a young child, so I decided to use it as the base for a self-portrait. The artwork combines present and past travels and childhood memories. I used a French *brocante* apron, cross-stitch elements and embroidery. I used two doilies to write some text about my childhood and experience to add into the piece, hand stitching the words onto them. There is also a pocket, with space for a folding book inside.

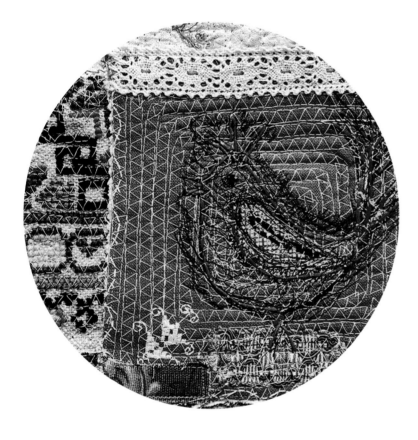

Above: Anne Kelly, *Self-Portrait* (detail), mixed-media textile.

Right: Anne Kelly, *Self-Portrait*, mixed-media textile.

Nigel Cheney: Decorated

Nigel Cheney exhibited 'Decorated – Tour of Duty' at the UK's 2019 Knitting and Stitching Shows. I was a gallery exhibitor at the Harrogate event where I saw this moving and personal collection, which is described here by Nigel:

'This body of work encompassed over five years of research and practical textile experiments that reflected on the ideas of loss and commemoration. It explored just what we mean by the term "decorated". 2017 saw the centenary of the death of my great-grandfather. Like many of those who served and died in the First World War, he was "decorated" with three medals.'

'The Naseby 11: Naseby is a rural village in the district of Daventry, Northamptonshire, close to the border of Leicestershire. It is six miles from the place of my birth and several of my relatives live there still. In the centre of the village is the "Naseby Lion", a war memorial paid for by subscriptions from the villagers and erected in 1921 to honour the 11 local men who died in the First World War. The second man from the village to die was Private Ernest Alfred Gamble of the 2nd Battalion Northamptonshire. He died on 8 July 1916 and is commemorated on the Thiepval Memorial [Picardy, France]. The map that is used on his "bodybag" sculpture actually came from the municipal museum in Coleraine [Northern Ireland] and was part of a board game.'

'Uniforms are designed to make everyone of the same rank and regiment equal. A military decoration is an award of medal and ribbon that denotes heroism. To decorate expresses the need to personalize or make more attractive. As transitional objects, we hold clothing to us to experience some sense of the person to whom they belonged. Mythologies are created through repairing, altering and embellishing these. As an embroiderer, the methods and tools I have at my disposal lend themselves to the act of repair. The making of the work has been a method to explore many of the questions that I have had about remembrance and sacrifice and of how people put themselves back together after experiencing a traumatic loss. For me, this is a domestic and highly personal act that is concerned with creating memories and retelling stories through colour, texture, materials and imagery.'

Nigel Cheney, *The Naseby 11* (detail), mixed-media textile.

Nigel Cheney, *The Naseby 11: Ernest Gamble*, mixed-media textile.

A 'Travelling Book'

Whilst teaching and speaking to Embroiderers' Guild groups around the UK, I had noticed a lovely group project called 'travelling books'. The idea is simple: to create a series of embroidered pages on a theme, done by members and passed around to create a group piece. I have seen many on my travels and was struck by the quality of one belonging to Ruth Airey from the Cornwall South group. It has a great range of nature-based themes, including birds, insects, plants and landscape; and it is wonderful to see so many techniques represented, including embroidery and felting, collage and appliqué. Ruth explains:

> 'When the embroidery group suggested we set up a travelling book project, I was eager to join in. My book has travelled around members within the group and other friends too. The first page is my own work and from there it has been passed on to others. Each page has been done with so much care – it has become a real treasure. The page tells where the person got her inspiration from: some are stories, some are just a little comment. I, in turn, have worked quite a lot of pages for other travelling books and I hope my work gives as much pleasure to the recipient as I get from my book.'

Travelling book from various members of the Cornwall South Embroiderers' Guild, collected and completed by Ruth Airey; mixed-media textiles.

Local Travels: A Shop Sketchbook

I like to make collages in mixed media for sketchbook work, complementing my textile practice. I decided to keep a small sketchbook of vintage shop fronts, showing the changing nature, in a nostalgic sense, of the English high street. I used a mixture of pen and ink drawing, paper collage and fabric ephemera glued over the outline to create the works. I also used watercolour to add colour to the composition. Finally, there was some stitching involved, to create interest and texture.

Anne Kelly, *Shop Book*, 'Books' page, mixed media on paper.

Anne Kelly, *Shop Book*, 'Haberdashery' page, mixed media on paper.

Travel Ephemera

Jane Audas is a London-based writer, curator and collector of ephemera. She explains:

> 'I collect paper things. Ephemera is often well-travelled pieces of paper that have survived just because: luggage tags that were never used, free booklets telling gentlemen how to pack, and poster stamps from far away department stores. For me such small things are redolent of travel, adventures and times that were (or seem, with hindsight) just that little bit more glamorous.'

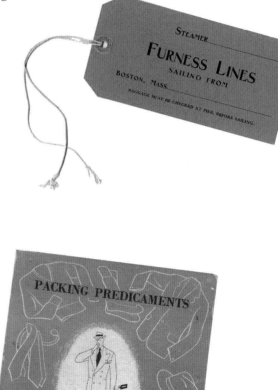

Jane has selected a few items connected with travel from her collection for this chapter. They are nostalgic and represent a more refined period of travel from days gone by. You can often find related items – maps, travel brochures and occasionally stickers or badges – in charity, junk or antique shops. They are useful as inspiration or to use in a mixed-media collage.

Vintage travel ephemera, collection of Jane Audas.

Chapter 5

Space and Exploration

*'I really believe in
the idea of the future.'*

Zaha Hadid, Iraqi-British architect

Travel Tags, various
contributors to
installation at the
Knitting and Stitching
Show, Olympia,
London 2018.

Space: inner and outer

When I was a child, space travel was all around us and we knew all the words connected with space flight – orbiting, splashdown, etc. The future seemed to be inevitably technological and space flight would be a big part of it. The future has turned out differently and 50 years on, we have not progressed as far as we had once thought we would. I have tried to capture here a variety of pieces that help us to connect with the idea of space. The moon reminds us of organic shapes and circular designs, on the earth as well as in the sky as we will explore in the work of several artists.

In the second part of this chapter, I will look at travel with a maritime theme. Boats and travel by boat have always fascinated me and have played a big part in my family's story. I was inspired to make a boat for a forthcoming solo exhibition at the Ruthin Craft Centre, North Wales, and to look into work related to travel and exploration.

Arrival sign on living wall, Singapore Changi Airport.

Anne Kelly, *Space Mood Board*, mixed media on board.

Exploring

1969 Dress

I used a simple shift dress as a background to make this piece, which commemorates the year of the first moon landing and my childhood memories of that time. It was the end of the sixties – an idealistic and eventful decade.

On the front of the work, there is a house and trees, harking back to my growing up in suburban Canada, as well as two planet-shaped circular pieces, one representing the moon and the other, again, representing home. The peacock is a reminder of a childhood vacation with my grandmother. All of this is interspersed with sixties-inspired trim.

On the reverse side is a large weather vane, a stitched piece that I found in a charity shop in Australia. There is a wreath and flowers representing garden and earth, and more houses to remind us of home.

The work was made in two parts, and each piece was stitched separately. They were then joined together in stitch and I hand-stitched around the appliquéd parts to emphasize their shapes.

Making an Embellished Garment

You can use a well-worn garment from your wardrobe or from a charity shop as a background for a piece of work. Select an easy shape – natural textiles are best – and avoid stretch fabric.

1 Choose the cloth that you would like to use to cover your garment with. I often make a small mood board to see how they work together.

2 Unpick the garment so that you can lay it out flat. Sleeves may need to be worked on separately.

3 When you have decided where to place the items, you can pin them to the background fabric and then stitch them on.

4 Finish by stitching the garment back together again. You can add trim and embellish the surface with hand embroidery at this stage.

Above: Anne Kelly, *1969 Dress* (front), mixed-media textile.

Below: Anne Kelly, *1969 Dress* (reverse, detail), mixed-media textile.

Betty Busby: Organelle

This piece by American textile artist Betty Busby takes a close-up look at cell structure, design and colour. It is a densely worked piece and tells us the story of organelles, as Betty explains:

'The bustling life of a living cell is carried on by various organelles which perform their discrete tasks. I used the natural formation of felted wool fibres to mimic the organic nature of the tiny city that lives within. The organelles within each cell carry out their designated tasks, from making energy out of food to processing proteins, through transcription and translation. The more closely we look at the way each of the billions of cells function, the miracle that is life becomes ever more apparent.'

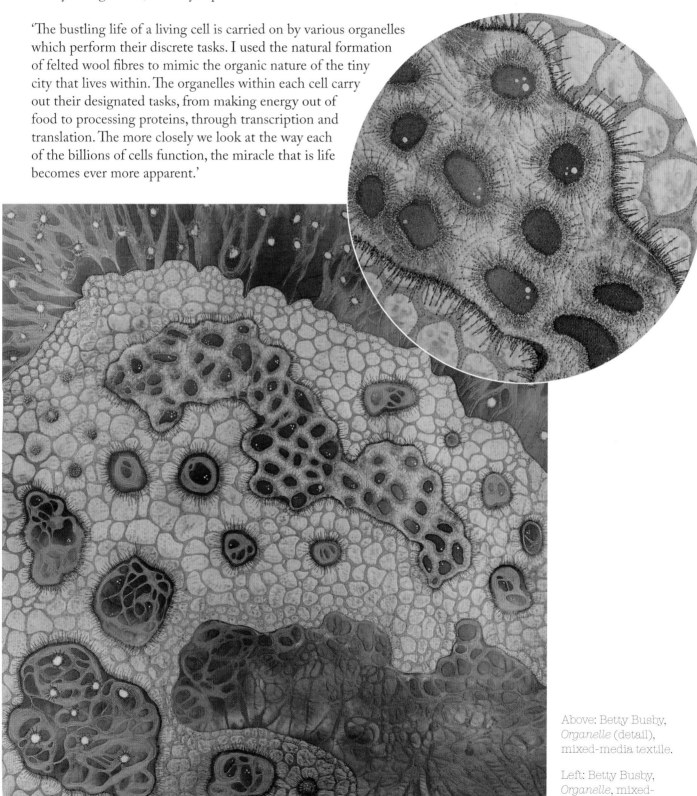

Above: Betty Busby, *Organelle* (detail), mixed-media textile.

Left: Betty Busby, *Organelle*, mixed-media textile.

Jenifer Newson and Susan Johanknecht: Crevice/Map

Crevice/Map is a collaborative project between book artist Susan Johanknecht and printmaker Jenifer Newson. It deals with relationships between internal and external landscapes, using imagery from Ordnance Survey maps and body organs. The text uses the language of geology and of a journey to describe the vulnerability of bodies and landscapes. One side of the book/map incorporates a poem by Susan, and the other a text derived from Jenifer's account of a climb up Ben Nevis.

The map is screen-printed and hand coloured with watercolour inks. It is housed in a fly-mesh slipcase. It has a lovely textural presence and the muted colours enable the viewer to appreciate the text. It is a great example of the power of combining text and imagery to create meaningful observations.

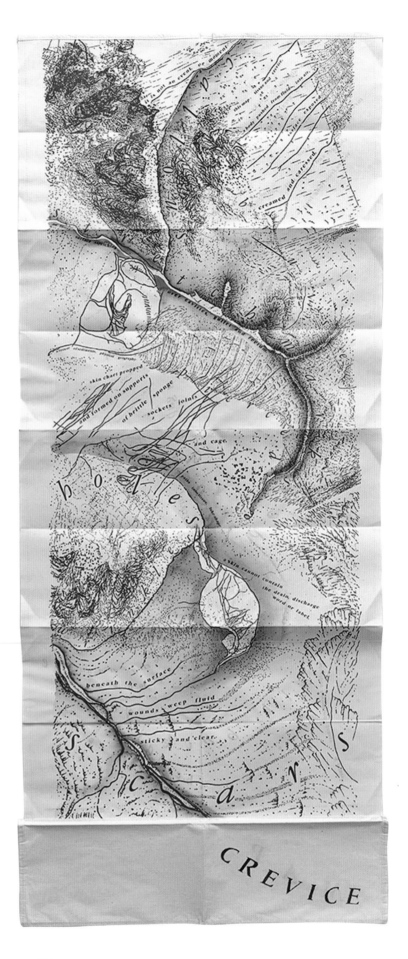

Jenifer Newson and
Susan Johanknecht,
Crevice/Map, hand-
coloured screen print.

Lizzie Farey: Luna

Lizzie Farey makes beautifully constructed willow sculptures. This piece is informed by her location in south-west Scotland, as she describes:

'*Luna*, meaning 'moon' in Latin, was inspired by the night sky. We have one of the largest expanses of dark sky in Europe, the Galloway Dark Sky Park. We even have our own "dark sky ranger" who will take you out stargazing or moon-watching. The area is mostly forests, glens, hills and lochs with very few buildings and even less light pollution. The area inspires my work, the sense of expansiveness and freedom but also a close relationship to the untamed nature of the area. I use willow that I grow here in Galloway to make the piece, forming the shapes with my hands before constructing the design.'

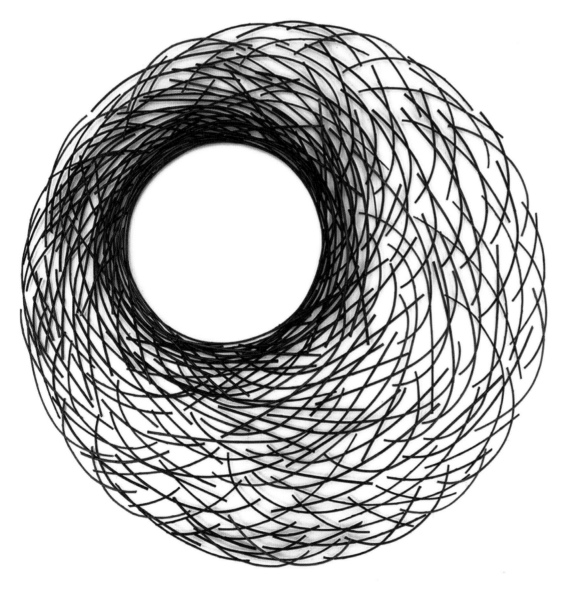

Lizzie Farey, *Luna*, willow sculpture.

Cynthia Pearson: City Lights

UK artist Cynthia Pearson's career in textiles began with a course in printed and woven textiles and she subsequently gained a distinction for the City and Guilds Embroidery Course. She has worked as a college lecturer and external assessor as well as Textile Artist in Residence at Bewdley Museum in Worcestershire, England. She regularly exhibits at the Royal Birmingham Society of Artists and local open studios.

Cynthia's work is always dependent on the intrinsic qualities of fabric and thread. She exploits the way in which light reflects on various surfaces. All of her textile pieces are a direct response to familiar surroundings. Nature, the changing times of day and the seasons are constant themes in her work. She was inspired to create *City Lights* by the photos that British astronaut Tim Peake took during his time on the International Space Station. She was also preparing work, at the time, for an exhibition based on maps.

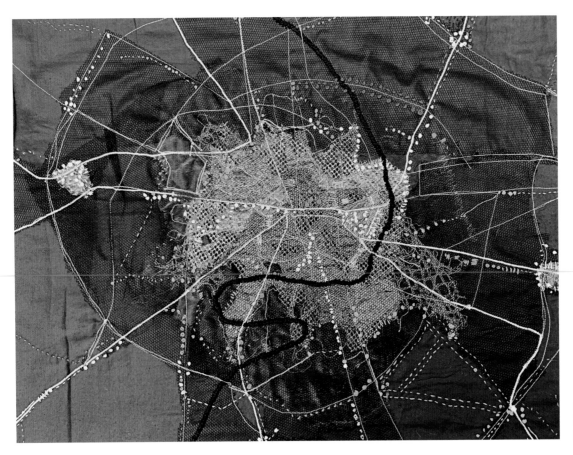

Cynthia Pearson, *City Lights*, mixed-media textile.

Nigel Cheney: Rabbit Moon

Nigel Cheney's work is featured in Chapter 4, but I also wanted to include an image of his night sky/moon work, which he describes in fascinating detail here:

'In a world of uncertainty, I take great comfort from looking at the moon on my ritual early morning walk to the swimming pool. On its constant cycle of waxing and waning it is always the full moon that inspires me most. Many years ago, I visited the anthropology museum in Mexico City and became fascinated by the ancient creation myths that talk of the relationship between rabbits and the moon. (Other cultures focus on romantic tales of the hare gazing at the moon and this in turn has been the drive behind many stitched textiles.)'

Nigel Cheney, *Rabbit Moon* (detail), mixed-media textile.

'In the summer of 2006, I was fortunate enough to spend six weeks on a research trip to Mexico. One of the most fascinating aspects of this trip was the visit to the Teotihuacan site and the pyramids of the sun and the moon. As I understand Aztec mythology, there is a belief that the universe is not permanent or everlasting, but subject to death like any living creature. However, even as it died, the universe would be reborn again into a new age, or "sun". In this particular legend, there were four creations; in each one, one god undertook the toil of being the sun: Quetzalcoatl, Tezcatlipoca, Tlaloc and Ehecatl. The Mesoamericans believed the moon grew to bear the mark of a rabbit.'

'I became captivated by this story, the duality of the two protagonists and their sacrifice, their similarities and their contrasts. I knew that I wanted to explore the possibility of working on two pieces simultaneously on the Schiffli [embroidery] machine and to pursue the idea of how stitch can transform cloth. By covering identical digital prints with either white or black machine threads I knew that there would be a dramatic disruption to the imagery on the cloth, but the excitement of the project was in how an overall stitch pattern could pull and distort an overall fabric in a very subtle way, providing a rich surface but with a minimal aesthetic.'

'In recent works it is often the underside of the work, where the stitches create seemingly random marks that are a discovery, rather than the accuracy of responding to the digital print of the original artwork, that I feel are most successful.'

Nigel Cheney, *Rabbit Moon*, mixed-media textile.

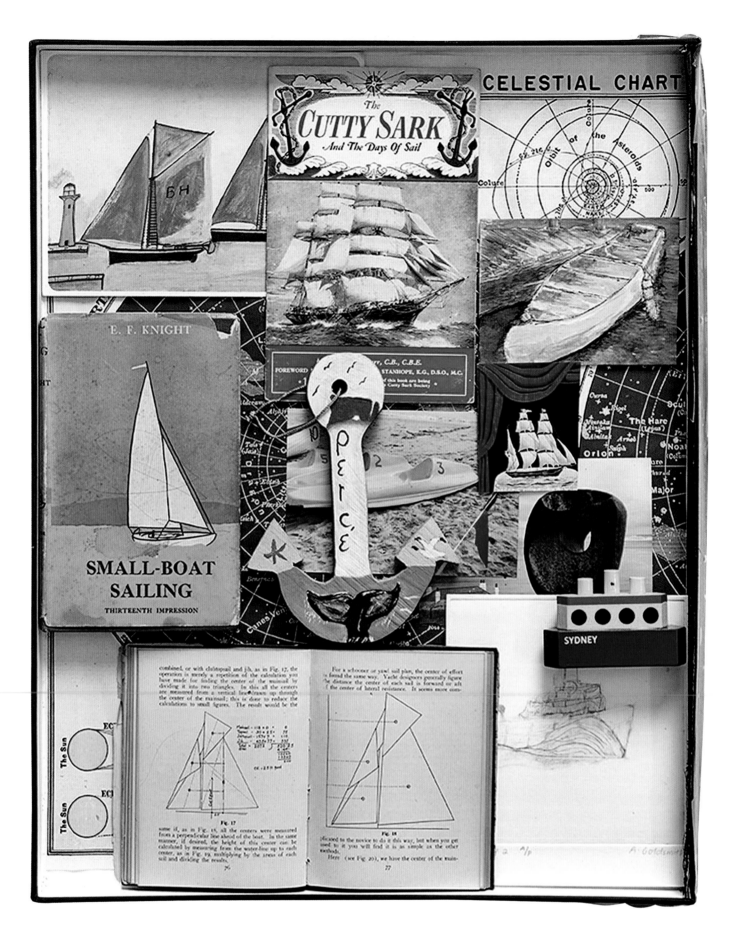

Anne Kelly, *Boat Mood Board*, mixed media on board.

Boats

I covered two found boats with pages from a vintage sailing instruction book. They were then varnished with a water-based varnish. The sails on the sailing boat were embellished with antique silk flag ribbons, gifted to me in Australia. I also used map fabric to complete the work and overstitched the pieces. They had to be attached to the sailboat's rigging and coaxed into place.

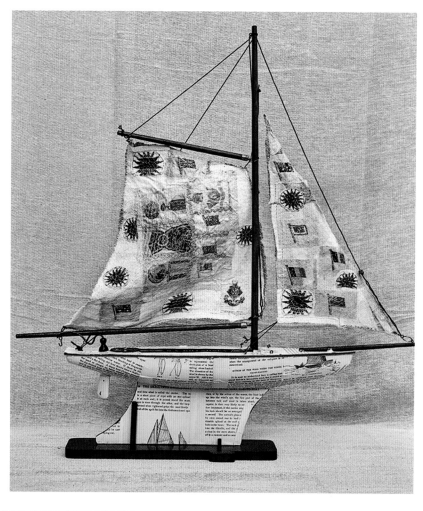

Right: Anne Kelly, *Sailing Boat*, mixed-media paper, textile and wooden boat.

Left: Anne Kelly, *Boat*, mixed-media paper and wooden boat.

Shelly Goldsmith: Locus of the Dress

Shelly Goldsmith is an artist who uses textile materials to interpret the emotions and memories associated with human experience. Using reclaimed garments, stories are recalled, imagined and retrieved; witness to the ever-evolving personal testimonies we all possess and carry around with us throughout our lives. I am drawn to the way that she combines internal and external themes, often in the same piece of work. Shelly tells us more:

> '*Locus of the Dress* brings together contemporary textiles and psychology in an exploration through a body of textile work depicting two locations: Margate's coast [south-east England] and Cincinnati, USA. I travel visually to these two locations to represent these extremes. Through my work I ask the question "Where on the continuum (the psychological theory 'Locus of Control') am I?"'

> 'The two pieces are from an investigation "Locus of the Dress", all produced through digital dye-sublimation printing processes on the inside surface of reclaimed garments (whole garment printing on women's dresses or dress fragments). In these pieces the inside elements, such as raw edges, loose threads on the back of embroidery, overlocked seams, etc., alert the viewer that they are witnessing the intimate side of the dress. The photographs are taken on walks along the Thanetian coast in Kent, along the powerful border where water meets land with the rhythm and predictability of the tides. The sea pool depicted in these pieces is the Walpole Bay tidal pool, Margate. Elements of [the series] have been shown in the UK and internationally.'

Shelly Goldsmith, *Locus of the Dress*, dye sublimation, mixed media

Shelly Goldsmith, *Locus of the Dress*, dye sublimation, mixed media.

Bettina Matzkuhn: Tides

Bettina Matzkuhn is a Canadian textile artist who uses stories about ecology, history and geography in her embroidered work. She has collaborated with people from other disciplines, such as meteorology and marine biology. She describes how one of her inspirations developed:

'One of my earliest memories is from when my father took me along on a trip to a sailmaker's loft in Vancouver. The light poured in through tall windows. Strips of fabric were laid out on an enormous hardwood floor. It had a few openings in it where women sat at sewing machines that were level with the floor, so that as they sewed the long strips together, the weight was supported. Bolts of cloth were stacked on shelves. At the window sat a man wearing a sailmaker's palm, sewing hanks onto the luff of a sail with heavy waxed thread. I was captivated.'

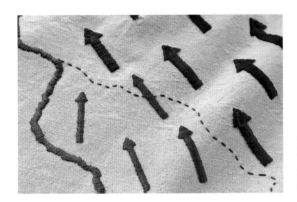

Bettina Matzkuhn, *Tides* (detail), mixed-media textile on sailcloth.

Bettina Matzkuhn, *Tides*, mixed-media textile on sailcloth.

'From 2010 to 2012 I researched the history of sails. I worked with a professional sailmaker who taught me the basics of their construction. Sails are wing-like, airfoil shapes. They are related to clothing, with tapered seams, faced edges, stiffening and reinforcing, eyelets and ties. I made a prototype, then four 12ft [3.6m] tall sets of cotton canvas sails. In my research I found that sails are often decorated. I hand-embroidered imagery from tide and pilot charts, cloud species and the endless patching required on long voyages. Specially formed wooden battens give a curve to each sail, and steel rigging with counterweights allow them to tilt slightly, implying we are underway.'

'My father was a devoted sailor and the series is an homage to his memory. From him, I gained a love for maps, geography and the natural world. To be a good sailor requires a personal knowledge about natural systems. It also entails communal knowledge, such as pilot and tide current charts, and information shared amongst locals: reefs, deadheads, rough water conditions, places where the wind is fierce. These systems of knowledge have parallels for other workers and travellers.'

An Unfinished Journey

I found a canoe on the internet – or to be more precise, a hand-hewn wooden skeleton of a canoe. I was looking for a canoe structure to cover as an installation piece for my forthcoming exhibition at Ruthin Craft Centre, North Wales. I found it on a selling/trading site called 'Preloved' and got in touch with the family who had advertised it.

It transpired that the children of the woman who had the piece hanging up in her garage had made it with their woodwork teacher at Ripon Grammar School, many years ago. When the item was completed, their family was entrusted with it. They attempted to cover it with marine ply, to make it seaworthy, but didn't succeed, so the canoe remained unfinished for many years. The adventure to collect it involved hiring a van and travelling up to Ripon in north-east England. The canoe had been sawn in half to get it into the van, and also to make it a more transportable size.

Canoe sections after
washing, in the
author's garden.

Anne Kelly, *Unfinished
Journey Boat*, mixed-
media textile, paper
and wooden boat.

When it was eventually back in my studio, we reassembled it to a more manageable shape. I then covered it with a combination of vintage embroidery patterns and textiles. The fabric was soaked in a 50/50 mixture of PVA glue and water, which was applied with a brush to cut strips. These were then wrapped around the skeleton of the boat and interspersed with other vintage fabric sections.

Anne Kelly, *Unfinished Journey Boat* (detail), mixed-media textile, paper and wooden boat.

Anne Kelly, *Unfinished Journey Boat* (detail), mixed-media textile, paper and wooden boat.

The boat is an allegory for the process of my emigration to the UK from Canada. When I was 21, I won two consecutive Elizabeth Greenshields Foundation Awards to travel to the UK from Canada. I made a new life in London and have lived, studied and worked in the UK ever since. This piece represents shedding the past comforts of home and making a new life abroad, as yet unfinished …

Anne Kelly, *Unfinished Journey Boat*, mixed-media textile, paper and wooden boat.

Cornwall Sea House Map

I made this map when on a teaching tour of Cornwall in the south-west of England. I found an old map in a charity shop and added some small embroideries of boats and houses, made out of fabric and map pieces. They were hand- and machine-stitched together. The piece was laminated, then stitched with machine embroidery and embellished. It evokes the Cornish landscape and countryside.

Anne Kelly, *Cornwall Sea House Map*, mixed-media textile and paper.

Kathryn Clark: Refugee Stories

Another contemporary textile artist looking at the sea and its impact on our current discourse is San Francisco-based Kathryn Clark, whose powerful series 'Refugee Stories' is timely in depicting the Syrian refugee crisis, as she explains:

> 'Inspired by the historical storyboard of the Bayeux Tapestry, "Refugee Stories" is a series of hand-stitched embroidery panels that follow the journey of the Syrian refugees into Europe. The monumental scale of the crisis, the second largest mass migration in history, is documented in various points along the refugees' journey out of Syria and into Western Europe. Each point along their journey was affected by geography: whether by sea or land, pastoral farmland or war-torn desert. Using international news stories, Google Earth and numerical data from the United Nations, each panel pieces together the journey in one schematic map.'

> 'In *By Sea (The Aegean)*, erratic loops of red stitching document the Syrian refugees' perilous journey from Turkey into Greece. The first leg of their journey is on small, crowded boats from mainland Turkey to the larger Greek islands of Lesvos, Chios, Samos and Kos. Once on Greek soil, the refugees continue their journey by ferry across the Aegean Sea into mainland Greece and onward by foot or train into Western Europe.'

Her work is moving and reminds us once again that not all journeys are planned or happy ones.

Kathryn Clark, *By Sea (The Aegean)*, mixed-media textile.

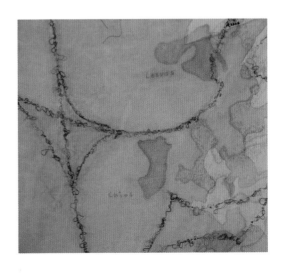

Kathryn Clark, *By Sea (The Aegean)* (detail), mixed-media textile.

Resources for Journeys

'And so a single thread can set a world in motion.'

Joan Miró, Spanish artist

Anne Kelly, *Box Collage*, mixed media in wooden box.

Working Away

In this section, we will look at some suggestions for working while travelling. There are ideas for paper and textile, and for using media and recording whilst you are away. A little bit of organizing before a journey enables you to work more productively and makes it easier to access materials to use when you feel like it.

Selection of travel-sized art materials, collection of the author.

Packing space is always a problem, especially when you want to bring sewing and art materials with you too. Fortunately, you can minimize this with a bit of planning and jettisoning of unnecessary items. Below are some ideas for travel and journey projects as well as basic paper collage and sewing kits, ideal for whether you are planning a trip around the world or around your town …

Anne Kelly, *Map Bag*, mixed-media textile on canvas bag.

Paper

I am starting with paper as it is probably the medium most commonly found on our travels, whether local or long distance, for example airline boarding passes, train and bus tickets, postage stamps, maps, postcards, luggage tags and stickers. I like to keep these objects for use later on, and I take a small plastic pouch with me where I can store them and keep them dry. I like to take a good set of watercolour- or ink-based coloured pencils to create background colour with. It is always less daunting to start with a base tone, and newspaper or thin tissue paper can be equally useful for this. Look for colourful or interesting patterns on brochures and publicity items, which are often free and can be torn out as part of your collage. Paper napkins, till receipts and tourist itineraries are all good for the background too.

Anne Kelly, *Park Walk Folding Book*, paper and watercolour with stitch.

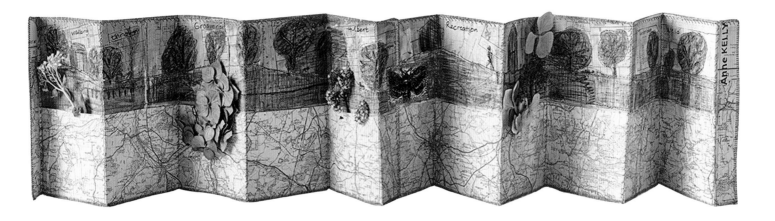

Sketchbook cover and drawing case, collection of the author.

Small Collages

I taught alongside the American artist Donna Watson in Australia and New Zealand a few years ago and enjoyed seeing her collaged work, based on the Japanese philosophy of *wabi-sabi*. She uses a limited colour palette and minimal stock of materials to great effect, often using items that you might gather on a journey, collected from near to her home and further away.

Basic paper collage kit for travel

» Plastic folder, A5/A4-sized for saving paper items

» Glue stick

» Coloured pencils – watercolour or ink-based are good

» Scissors – small, but not in hand luggage

Donna Watson, *Hope*, mixed media on card.

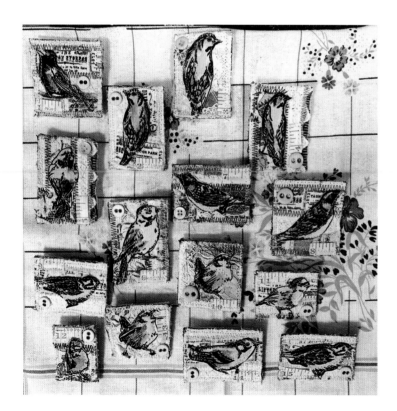

Anne Kelly, *Bird Badges*, works in progress in the author's studio.

Making a Travel Paper Collage

1 Distress or wash your paper background with a tone – this will make it less scary to work on!

2 Select your items for collage, making sure that they are flat and not too thick. I often separate cardboard items, taking off the top few layers.

3 Play with your objects, arranging them in different formats until you are happy with your composition.

4 Glue your items down; remember a torn edge can be beautiful, and using thin handmade paper or tissue paper in some areas is also quite effective.

Mapping Home

Tiel Seivl-Keevers is a multi-disciplinary Australian artist who also creates paintings and mixed-media works on paper. As curator Laura Brinin says, she 'uncovers another memory of a journey on foot through the Australian landscape'. Talking about her 'Dust' series, Tiel says:

'I created 25 of these paper collages for a group exhibition earlier this year titled "Dust". I have a love for the handmade and particularly ceramics so I wanted to make something that would link our work together. I always keep scraps of paper – in fact I have drawers full of paper as I collect or buy papers when travelling for my art practice. As a way of utilizing these, I manipulated the surface with acrylic and ink and various other techniques I use when painting. I then cut out the shapes and mounted them onto a background. Each one is framed individually with the intention that they would be hung in pairs or small groups.'

Anne Kelly, *Park Walk* (detail), mixed media on paper.

Tiel Seivl-Keevers, *Dust*, paper, collages, mixed media on paper.

Cloth

Once you start to see how cloth is so different in every country in the world, you start to appreciate the myriad examples of it everywhere you look. It is often the small pieces that inspire me, which is useful when touring as there's not a lot of available baggage space. I like to look in charity shops and markets when visiting new places. Lace and embroidery vary widely too and you can find amazing samples of it when travelling. I often take partially completed pieces with me to work on as it is good to have something started. Another idea would be to make neutrally coloured, blank book forms that you can add drawings and stitch to once you arrive at your destination or when you decide on your subject matter.

Unfinished Indian embroidery from Satguru, Jaipur.

Anne Kelly, *Australians*, mixed-media textile.

Collecting 'Souvenirs'

Indian bazaars and Moroccan markets spring to mind when I think about colour overload and having too much choice, but there is also something satisfying about working with pieces that you find in charity shops or on the ground when out on a walk. As we saw with Debbie Lyddon's work in Chapter 4, she is masterful at capturing one shape or element in the landscape, and it is this approach that can make travel or journey-inspired pieces so effective.

Anne Kelly, *China Garden* (detail), mixed-media textile.

Anne Kelly, *Japanese Teapots* (detail), mixed-media textile.

Basic sewing kit for travel

This will depend on your chosen method and techniques. I like to take a pouch with the following:

» Needles

» Embroidery cotton

» Small fabric scissors or thread cutter

» Plain fabric to work on

» Backing fabric for stability

» Some ribbon

» Buttons if desired

Below: Anne Kelly, *Corali* (detail), mixed-media textile.

Left: Anne Kelly, *Tree of Life Bag*, mixed-media textile on canvas bag.

Media and Recording

In the past, travel involved taking photos of everything and having many albums stored from journeys. Since the advent of digital photography, we can be instantly selective in what we take and how we store it. Photos can be a wonderful reference for making drawings and studies from. I like to crop and alter photos soon after I take them so that they are ready to use.

It is possible to trace images directly from a screen, but it is better to print them out and use them on paper or as part of a collage. (I always advise students to test images before using them with water-based media, in case the inks run.)

Anne Kelly, *Boston Postcard*, mixed media on card.

Anne Kelly, *Bristol Postcard*, mixed media on card.

Drawings from photos can help us to remember forgotten details. In *Montreal Collage*, I have juxtaposed images of Montreal with paper items found there and photographs taken on a visit to the city.

Anne Kelly, *Montreal Collage*, mixed media on card.

Conclusion

'Two roads diverged in a wood, and I – I took the one less travelled by, And that has made all the difference.'

Robert Frost, American poet

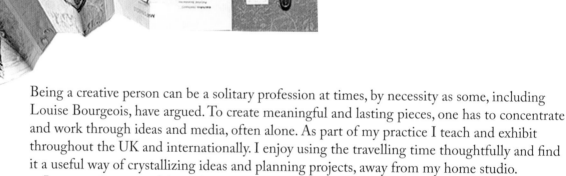

Being a creative person can be a solitary profession at times, by necessity as some, including Louise Bourgeois, have argued. To create meaningful and lasting pieces, one has to concentrate and work through ideas and media, often alone. As part of my practice I teach and exhibit throughout the UK and internationally. I enjoy using the travelling time thoughtfully and find it a useful way of crystallizing ideas and planning projects, away from my home studio.

In my exploration of this subject I enjoyed seeing how others have distilled their visions of smaller and larger spaces, near and far, in their artworks. There are so many exciting and inspirational places to work from – they surround us everywhere. It is humbling and heartening when I travel across the world to see the connections made through my work and writing by other makers and practitioners. Equally, I am privileged to work with many talented individuals and groups at home in the UK.

We are faced with immediate challenges in the ways in which we now choose to travel – our 'carbon footprint' has never been so important. Documenting the changes in our natural environment will become ever more vital and meaningful. The social upheaval that is a product of environmental change has been touched upon in this book and in my previous book, *Textile Folk Art*. We are bombarded with information about how we can influence the situation and it is often difficult to assimilate all of these changing briefings.

I hope that this book will encourage creativity and travel through making and stitching – that is true 'emotional repair', to reference Louise Bourgeois again. Taking 'the road less travelled' can also lead to new discoveries and independence. My family and friends have understood and supported me throughout these life journeys, both internal and external. Here I have shown and suggested ways of starting your creative journeys and how to work in different media when travelling. It is time to go and explore …

Above: Anne Kelly,
China Garden, mixed-
media textile.

Opposite: Anne Kelly,
Australian Sketchbook,
mixed media.

Featured Artists
and Contributors

Ruth Airey
Brooke Atherton · www.brookeathertonart.com
Jane Audas · www.janeaudas.com
Vanessa Barragão · www.vanessabarragao.com
Linda Bassett · Instagram @libertylindylou
Catherine Blackburn · www.catherineblackburn.com
Betty Busby · www.bbusbyarts.com
Nigel Cheney · www.nigelcheney.com
Kathryn Clark · www.kathrynclark.com

Lizzie Farey · www.lizziefarey.co.uk
Ali Ferguson · www.aliferguson.co.uk
Shelly Goldsmith · www.shellygoldsmith.com
Heidi Hankaniemi · www.hedihankaniemi.com
Amanda House · www.amanda-house.com
Susan Johanknecht · www.gefnpress.co.uk
Ekta Kaul · www.ektakaul.com
Zachari Logan · www.zachariloganart.com
Debbie Lyddon · www.debbielyddon.co.uk

Anne Kelly, *Japanese Kettles*, mixed-media textile.

For Investigation

Amano Museum, Lima, Peru
www.eng.museoamano.org

Anokhi Museum of Hand Printing, Jaipur, India
www.anokhi.com/museum/home.html

Art Gallery of Nova Scotia, Halifax, Canada
www.artgalleryofnovascotia.ca

Cape Dorset Arts, Canada
www.dorsetfinearts.com

Compton Verney Art Gallery and Park, Compton Verney, Warwickshire
www.comptonverney.org.uk

The Embroiderers' Guild UK
www.embroiderersguild.com

London Transport Museum, Covent Garden, London
www.ltmuseum.co.uk

Mississippi Valley Textile Museum, Almonte, Ontario, Canada
www.mvtm.ca

Museum of Art + Craft, Ditchling, East Sussex
www.ditchlingmuseumartcraft.org.uk

The Postal Museum, Mount Pleasant, London
www.postalmuseum.org

Sea Acres Rainforest Centre, Port Macquarie, NSW, Australia
www.nationalparks.nsw.gov.au/things-to-do/visitor-centres/sea-acres-rainforest-centre

Society for Embroidered Work
www.societyforembroideredwork.com

Te Papa Museum, Wellington, New Zealand
www.tepapa.govt.nz

Timeless Textiles, Newcastle, NSW, Australia
www.timelesstexiles.com.au

Tunbridge Wells Museum and Art Gallery, Tunbridge Wells, Kent
(reopening in 2021/2012 as The Amelia at the Amelia Scott)
Instagram @theamelia_tw

West Country Embroiderers
www.westcountryembroiderers.co.uk

Anne Kelly, *Sea Acres Sketchbook*, mixed media.

Further Reading

Aoki, Kazuko, *Embroidered Garden Flowers*, Roost Books, 2017

Brotton, Jerry and Millea, Nick, *Talking Maps*, The Bodleian Library, 2019

Brunt, Peter *et al*, *Oceania*, Royal Academy of Arts, 2018

Hamilton, Laurie, *The Painted House of Maud Lewis*, Goose Lane Editions, 2001

Harmon, Katharine, *You are Here: Personal Geographies and Other Maps of the Imagination*, Princeton Architectural Press, 2003

Hazell, Rachel, *Bound*, Octopus Publishing Group, 2018

Holmes, Cas and Kelly, Anne, *Connected Cloth*, Batsford, 2013

Kelly, Anne, *Textile Folk Art*, Batsford, 2018

Kelly, Anne, *Textile Nature*, Batsford, 2016

Taillandier, Yvon, *Joan Miró: I Work Like a Gardener*, Princeton Architectural Press, 2017

Anne Kelly, table display for a talk.

Suppliers

UK

Bernina UK
91 Goswell Road
London EC1V 7EX
020 7549 7849
www.bernina.com

Colouricous (block printing)
Unit 7, Alma Industrial Estate
Chesham HP5 3HB
0203 362 4114
www.colouricious.com

Seawhite
Avalon Court,
Star Road Trading Estate
Partridge Green
Horsham RH 13 8RY
01403 711633
www.seawhite.co.uk

Shepherds
30 Gillingham Street
London SW1V 1HU
020 7233 9999
www.store.bookbinding.co.uk

George Weil
Old Portsmouth Road
Peasmarsh
Guildford GU3 1LZ
01483 565800
www.georgeweil.com

North America

Blick Art Materials
PO Box 1267
Galesburg, IL 61402-1267
1-800-828-4548 USA
1-309-343-6181 Ext. 5402
International
www.dickblick.com

PRO Chemical and Dye
126 Shove Street
Fall River, MA 02724
1-800-228-9393
www.prochemicalanddye.com

Australia and New Zealand

The Thread Studio
6 Smith Street
Perth, WA 6000
(61) 8 9227 1561
www.thethreadstudio.com

Minerva
237 Cuba Street
Wellington
New Zealand
04 934 3424
www.minerva.co.nz

Art Textile Courses

UK

Cowslip Workshops
www.cowslipworkshops.co.uk

Hope and Elvis
www.hopeandelvis.com

Needle and Thread Workshops
www.needleandthreadworkshops.com

Selvedge
www.selvedge.org/collections/
workshops

West Dean College of Arts and
Conservation
www.westdean.org.uk

USA and Canada

French General
www.frenchgeneral.com/collections/
workshops

Maiwa School of Textiles
www.schooloftextiles.com

Australia and New Zealand

Berry Quilting Retreat
www.berryquiltingretreat.com.au

Grampians Textures
www.grampianarts.com.au/grampians-
textures.html

The Happenstore
www.thehappenstore.com

Fibrearts New Zealand
www.fibreartsnz.co.nz

Anne Kelly, *Irene's Garden* (detail) from commission, mixed-media textile.

Anne Kelly, *Beetles*,
mixed-media textile with
author's sewing kit.

Acknowledgements

My thanks to the artists, makers and contributors named in the text. Their details are in
Featured Artists and Contributors.

Special thanks are due to my editors Tina Persaud and Nicola Newman at Batsford for their
support of this project. A big thank you to Rachel Whiting for her luminous photography.

To my father Harry, who can't remember all of our journeys, but I do.

For my family, especially Paul, and our past and future travels together.

Index